CLASSROOM PORTFOLIO
OF
ENERGIZERS, PUZZLES, QUIZZES, GAMES AND BRAIN TEASERS

CLASSROOM PORTFOLIO
OF
ENERGIZERS, PUZZLES, QUIZZES, GAMES AND BRAIN TEASERS

Fred B. Chernow and Carol Chernow

A number of the original illustrations in this book
were prepared by Lynne Chernow.

Parker Publishing Company, Inc.
West Nyack, New York

© 1979, *by*

PARKER PUBLISHING COMPANY, INC.

West Nyack, N.Y.

Library of Congress Cataloging in Publication Data

Chernow, Fred B.
  Classroom portfolio of energizers, puzzles, quizzes,
games, and brain teasers.

  Includes index.
  1. Games. 2. Puzzles. 3. Creative activities and
seatwork. I. Chernow, Carol,   joint author.
II. Title.
GV1203.C33   372.1'3   78-13377
ISBN 0-13-136291-7

Printed in the United States of America

We dedicate this book with much love and affection to our two daughters, Barbara and Lynne. Many of these puzzles and games we used with them as they were growing up. The more difficult brain teasers tried years ago helped them get admitted to their present schools—Brown and Cornell Universities.

Previous Books . . .

Teaching and Administering the High School Education Program, by Fred B. Chernow and Harold Genkin

School Administrator's Guide to Managing People, by Fred B. Chernow and Carol Chernow

School Administrator's September-June Almanac, by Fred B. Chernow and Carol Chernow

The Unique, Practical Value
This Book Offers

This portfolio will help you make your classroom a stimulating place for every pupil. By using this book often you will help your pupils to become more attentive and more responsive, and to raise their achievement level. They will be enthusiastic about school because you will capture their attention and stimulate their interest in learning and problem solving. There are over 200 classroom-tested games, energizers, and puzzles to vitalize every subject, illustrate difficult concepts, excite reluctant learners, and generate enthusiasm for learning. For example, Chapter 7 alone offers 16 science activities to arouse your pupils' curiosity about the world around them.

A lively collection of activities, mini-lessons, and brain teasers, this handy volume provides everything you need to turn your classroom into an animated, fun-filled place where learning takes place and pupils are encouraged to use their potential. Brimming with provocative, proven games, quizzes, and energizers, this treasury of varied and practical ideas can be used daily in your classroom. In the first chapter you will find at your fingertips 15 listening skills ideas that are easy to understand and readily put to use. In subsequent chapters you will find teaching ideas that tie in perfectly with your pupils' varied learning levels in reading, math, spelling, and social studies. These are supplemented with an inexhaustible supply of attention-getting devices and teaching games based on creative writing, health learning, natural environment, consumer economics, metric measurement, and career education.

This compendium is invaluable to teachers who want to create a relaxed, tension-free environment that will arouse their pupils' sense of discovery and encourage them to apply themselves in a constructive, *self*-satisfying manner. The detailed techniques, models, and ideas will help teachers reach their pupils more quickly and effectively. Pupils with short attention spans will love the dozens of games and puzzles. The more able pupils will look forward to the brain teasers and quizzes. For example, there are pupil-made board games for four players, such as Urban Geography, as well as whole class activities like Curtain Call and individual energizers called Challenge Cards. All your pupils will respond to the many devices that will add sparkle to your lessons. This veritable galaxy of games and subject area stimulants will bring out the best efforts and qualities of your pupils.

You will also find the portfolio organized for easy use. Every major subject area is covered and the easy-to-use format includes activities for every grade level. For example, Chapter 3 contains ideas for making reading fun. There are games and puzzles for *all* elementary grades. Their high interest level makes them applicable to any age or grade level. Current, relevant themes are used throughout. Chapter 5 helps you teach the metric system, and again there are stimulating ideas for all grade levels. If you have a bright class you can use the suggestions for the next grade level. Slow learners can benefit from the suggestions given for a lower level. *Every* idea can be used or easily adapted for all students in your class. All the suggestions have been carefully selected from ideas proven to be successful in a variety of situations. The portfolio arrangement makes finding what you need simple and foolproof. Each of the 13 chapters is devoted to a single subject area. Specific ideas are set apart and illustrated, when necessary, for your easy adaptation.

A host of motivational games, culminating quizzes, and "do-now" activities make this book an inseparable companion to your lesson plans or teacher's manual. You can use it every day to raise the instructional level of your class.

Are you looking for ways to introduce consumer education? Chapter 9 will give you a score of simulations and games you can introduce. Want to teach the basic number facts without putting your class to sleep? Read Chapter 4 and you'll be raring to go. Would you like some short "board work" assignments that will keep your pupils meaningfully occupied while you tally the attendance? Every chapter has several of these "do now" activities that you can use for this purpose.

You will find these puzzles, games, and brain teasers to be exactly what you need for making *all* your pupils interested in the lesson. Gone will be the feeling that you have lost half the class. You'll have 200 ready-to-go activities to evoke pupil interest and attention.

Here is just a sampling of the many exciting new approaches to be found in this portfolio:

- Activities which challenge able students so that they do not become bored.
- Methods for making the slow learner or special education youngster feel he or she is part of the mainstream.
- Motivation techniques that pique your pupils' interest in the lesson that follows.
- Enrichment activities that faster pupils can pursue on their own when they finish the regular assignment.
- Fillers to keep the class happily busy when just a few minutes remain before lunch or some other activity.
- Energizers that really work when you're dealing with "difficult children."
- Games that awaken hidden talents in your pupils.

In addition, you'll find dozens of little pointers that will stir the creativity of both teacher and pupil. You will begin to save valuable class time the day you begin using the book. You will be pleased with your ability to teach the standard subjects in a refreshingly different way. Your own thinking will be stimulated, and each lesson will be new as you capture the attention of the entire class. At the end of the day you will feel challenged and find yourself looking forward to what you can try tomorrow.

This unique book containing scores of teaching ideas will evoke positive feelings in you that will transfer quickly to the children you teach. Both you and your class will benefit from the exciting new approaches that will characterize your school day. Lessons will take on an animation and vitality that will make your students sit up and notice. Here in a single volume is an extraordinary invitation to exciting discovery and adventure in your classroom.

The Authors

TABLE OF CONTENTS

CLASSROOM PORTFOLIO
OF
ENERGIZERS, PUZZLES, QUIZZES, GAMES AND BRAIN TEASERS

—1—

ACTIVITIES THAT INCREASE LISTENING SKILLS

Is listening the same as hearing? No. We hear many sounds but we don't always listen carefully. In this chapter you will find a host of listening games and activities that will help you sharpen the listening skills of your pupils. You will help them become "sound detectives" as they identify and discriminate between sounds. Various ear games will show you how to reward careful listening.

Among the various outcomes of these easy-to-copy listening lessons are: listening to understand relationships, listening for a purpose, sharpening pupils' ability to follow oral directions, and making pupils aware of the sounds around them.

Some of the mini-lessons and games will help you spark language arts lessons and also get your pupils ready for more sophisticated oral language and speech work.

There is a classification quiz and cause and effect game that will amuse your pupils as well as make them more alert.

Classification Quiz

AIM: *To listen for and understand relationships.*

Say aloud a group of words in which one word does not belong to the group. For example:

car   train   bus   bicycle   toy

Toy is the answer, because it is not a means of transportation.

tulip   grass   rose   dandelion   daisy

Grass is the answer, as used in the sense of a lawn without flowers.

Other groupings using words with which urban pupils may be more familiar may be used. Help the children listen carefully for the relationship between the words and determine the category to which they belong. Then have them select the unrelated word.

Have the pupils make up their own groups of words that belong together according to some means of classification.

Bring in groups of objects which by some criteria can be classed together; for example, round shape, particular color, function. Ask the children to bring in objects and explain what they have in common.

Write on the chalkboard four headings that will form major classifications, such as animals, trees, cities, pets. Divide the class into four teams, and assign each of them to a heading. Then allow each team in turn one minute to name as many items as they can that would fit under their heading. The game may be repeated by assigning the team to different headings. They can use their lists to test other teams by adding one word that does not belong.

Listening Triad

AIM: *To sharpen pupils' ability to follow oral directions.*

Here are three quickie energizers that you can use to fill in a few minutes while waiting for the lunch bell to ring.

1. Tape record a series of three to five simple directions, such as, "Walk around your chair once, then go to the window, then to the chalkboard and pick up a piece of chalk." Have a child or group of children follow the directions after hearing the series only once. As the children become more adept at listening to directions and following them in sequence, the directions could be to make a simple object or to fold paper in a certain way. Ask the children what they did in sequence. Have the children make up a series of simple directions and tape them for others to follow.

2. Tell a story with a sequence of sounds instead of words. Tape the sounds ahead of time, or perhaps the children could help develop a sequence of sounds that would tell a story.

3. Read to the class several short paragraphs involving a sequence of events. At a climactic point in the passage, invite the listeners to predict the next event and the final outcome. List all reasonable suggestions on the chalkboard. Have the children discuss the relative possibilities of each suggestion before deciding on the most probable turn of events. Then conclude the activity by reading the rest of the passage and revealing to the class what actually happened.

Be Specific!

AIM: *To listen for specific information.*

Read aloud once the statement given in A below. Then read aloud one at a time the statements in B. Ask the children to decide if the statements are true or false and to give reasons for their opinion. Do the same for the second group.

A.   1. George Washington traveled many times on horseback.
     2. He was a general and a president.
     3. His home was at Mt. Vernon in Virginia.
     4. He led a successful attack at Trenton, New Jersey.

B. 1. All Americans liked George Washington. (False)
    2. Washington was a good hunter. (False)
    3. His men won a battle at Trenton. (True)
    4. Washington loved to ride his horse. (False)

Point out that while some of the above statements may be true, in this exercise they can only be considered TRUE if the *specific* information is given in the four statements under column A.

Try this group of more personal statements.

A. 1. Two of the pupils in this room were late recently.
    2. At least one person likes to help me clean up the room.
    3. Three pupils are still working on their spelling.
    4. One person forgot to bring back the report card.

B. 1. Three pupils like spelling. (False)
    2. Two pupils have been late to class. (True)
    3. Spelling takes a long time to finish. (False)
    4. No one forgot to bring her/his report card. (False)

Now have a group of three or four pupils make up groups of statements to try out on the whole class.

Cause and Effect

AIM: *To provide practice in listening for causal relationships.*

1. Collect magazine pictures of people or animals in unusual situations. Show the picture briefly and then ask a pupil to describe what he or she saw. Ask other pupils to speculate about how the situation came about. After some practice, show the picture only to the child who is going to describe it. In this way, only listening skills will be tested.

2. Tell a simple story to the class. Then discuss the ending of the story with them and help them to understand the specific qualities of the characters, the situations, and the events that brought about that particular ending. Many well-known stories, such as the "Three Little Pigs," could be used.

3. Present situations and ask the children to guess about the possible causes and possible effects. For example, "When I left home this morning, I saw two people standing alongside their automobile which was parked on the side of the road. Why do you suppose they were parked there?" Encourage the pupils to present situations and speculate about causes. Or speculate with the children about, "What would happen if. . . ."

4. Ask a good reader to select three books from the class library shelf. Have him read aloud only the last page from each book. After the final page has been read, ask the reader to select volunteers who would like to tell the class what they think each book was about.

5. Ask pupils to supply another ending to a popular story with which they are familiar. Remind them that their ending must make sense based on the facts presented in the story. Have other pupils decide which ending makes more sense, based purely on logic. Which ending is more romantic?

Number Please

AIM: *To recognize and overcome poor listening habits.*

Read to the children a list of numbers and then ask them to select a particular one and respond orally.
Examples:

4-9-6-3	—What was the third number?
11-9-7-6-3	—Which number was the largest?
8-5-9-4	—Which number is closest to the sum of five plus five?

Tell the pupils that they must listen purposefully and selectively. Give the directions only once, and only after the series of numbers has been given. Items other than numbers can be used in this activity. For example, the children might be given a list or a sentence and asked to listen for the action words, or the names of countries or of cities, or the words that begin with a certain letter. Give only enough exercises for the child to see that it is difficult to select the correct answer when he doesn't know what he is to listen for. Then repeat the activity, this time telling the pupils what they are to do before they hear the series or the sentence.

Continue giving exercises until the children can select the correct answer nearly every time. Discuss with the pupils the reasons why they were more successful during the second part of the activity than they were during the first, eliciting from them the conclusion that when one knows in advance what he is to listen for, he usually listens more effectively.

Give short quizzes, based on listening, that the children can score themselves. It might be a quiz based on last night's TV show or an assembly program that everyone shared.

Tell your class before a guest speaker arrives that they will be quizzed on his or her remarks. Watch those ears perk up!

Listen Books

AIM: *To listen with a purpose.*

Who says that you can't have anything tangible from a listening experience! Your class can make a listen book. Here's how: Let us assume that your classroom has six rows of pupil desks. Play a tape-recorded story for the class. Find out how many minutes the tape or record runs. Divide that time by the number of pupil rows or clusters of desks. Give each row the responsibility for interpreting a certain segment of the story. Give each child in the room a piece of drawing paper. As children listen to their segment they draw a picture that illustrates what they are hearing.

For example, Row One draws anything they hear from the first five minutes of a thirty-minute tape. Row Two draws a picture from the second five-minute segment, etc.

After the tape or record has been played, collect the pictures from the entire class. A committee of children selects the best picture from each segment and assembles a picture book that illustrates the tape or record. Sequencing is important as they try to arrange their pictures in a logical manner. They may find that there are two or three good pictures from the same time segment. They can include all of them, thus making a more complete picture story.

This activity also motivates many children to read the book. They like to compare the artist's pictures with their own and write appropriate sentences to accompany their pictures.

So, they have listened with a purpose and you have something concrete to show for it.

Ear Games

AIM: *To reward careful listening.*

Here is a clutch of brief games that you can play to reinforce good listening habits.

1. Use such words as hop, jump, skip, slide. Say the action word first, then the name of the child who is to respond. Or divide the group into several sections, each section doing an action.

2. When it is time for children to get their coats, whisper one child's name softly. That child responds accordingly—rising to line up, getting his wraps, or raising his hands. The game demands both listening and watching, for the formation of the teacher's mouth in

saying a name helps children to recognize names. If the children get restless after a time, give a general word such as "boys," "girls," "everyone."

3. Use triangle, drum or rhythm sticks for this one. The teacher taps any number from one to six, asks "How many?", then adds a child's name for responses. Calling a child's name first relaxes other children's listening. After using this game several times, the teacher may choose a child to be the "teacher" and allow this pupil to choose the number, tap it out on the instrument, then call on someone to respond. Later the game may be extended to the use of number cards, having a child choose correctly the number that matches the taps he or she heard. As children become familiar with the numbers, extend the activity to higher numbers.

4. A variation of reading names at roll call may be the singing of a child's name. Then have the pupil sing the same little tune back to the teacher. This activity serves to identify both children who have unusual singing ability and conversely those who have not been exposed to preschool singing experiences and cannot repeat a tune.

5. Pupils are seated in a group. The teacher says a three-digit number, then points to a child and says, "Repeat it." The three digits must be repeated in correct order. Gradually move on to four digits, then five. Vary the game by using letters.

Sound Detective

AIM: *To identify and discriminate between sounds.*

Choose one child to be leader and another child, who is blindfolded, to be the "Sound Detective." The leader points to a member of the class who asks in a normal voice, "What is my name?" If the blindfolded pupil makes the proper identification, the person identified becomes the new Sound Detective. After a few minutes of this, go on to the next part of this activity.

Direct the pupils to close their eyes and listen to and identify particular sounds, such as a person walking, a book closing, paper crumpling, water running, pencil sharpener working, a drawer closing, coins jingling, or chalk on the board. Lead the children to a discussion of situations in which the identification of sounds is especially important. Any one pupil who identified all of the above sounds is promoted to "Chief of Detectives."

Read a story to the class and choose particular pupils to produce appropriate sound effects (sirens, horns, train whistles, etc.), to underscore the story line. This activity may be repeated from time to time until all the children have participated.

Words and Music

AIM: *To listen for and understand relationships.*

Play a record or a tape recording of a folk song. Ask: What is the message? How do the melody, the background notes, and the rhythm relate to the message? What is the mood of the music? Does it fit the message?

Ask the pupils to listen for a specified period of time to the theme songs and sound effects of commercials and programs on TV. Then have them analyze in class the relationship between the sound effects and the content of the program or commercial. Do the sound effects reflect the point of the program? Do they create attitudes or stimulate reactions in the listener? If so, how? Is the appeal obvious or subtle? The discussion might be extended to include the function of piped music in supermarkets and dentists' offices.

Have the pupils see a TV or movie adaptation of some book or story they have read. Point out how the screen writer, the visual effects director, and the sound effects director have selected material from the story, used it, and omitted other parts.

In what way has the dialog been changed?
Why are special effects used for some scenes and not others?
How does the addition of music and sound effects change your
    understanding of the story?

Straighten Out

AIM: *To listen for and understand relationships.*

Read a story to the class. Then without reading the story a
second time, show the pupils a jumbled series of illustrations that
depict scenes, characters, and events from the reading. Have the
children arrange the pictures in their proper order according to events
in the story. If such a picture file is not available, pictures from old,
to-be-discarded story books can be used for this purpose.

Have the class pantomime a nursery rhyme. Then reverse
some aspects of the order and discuss the effects with the class.

Read aloud:

Mary ate breakfast, went to school, woke up, and brushed
her teeth.

Ask, "What is wrong with that sentence?" "Why is it
wrong?" "How can it be fixed?"

Write the following words on the chalkboard and read them to
the children:

ball,   hit,   the,   Jim

Ask the children to orally arrange the words so that they make
sense. The three best arrangements (Jim hit the ball, the ball hit Jim,
hit the hall, Jim) should be discussed in terms of the relationship
between the word order and the meaning. Ask the class to make up

their own word puzzles using a series of words like this one. They can test each other.

Loaded Words

AIM: *To listen for and evaluate supporting material.*

Explain to the pupils that "loaded" words are those that affect the implications of a statement without changing the factual accuracy of its content. Then read aloud a group of headlines such as the following:

Yankees Slaughter Mets 3-1
Yankees Defeat Mets 3-1
Yankees Eke By Mets 3-1

Do all three headlines state the same information? What is the listener expected to infer in the first and third statements?

Ask the pupils to listen carefully for loaded words or statements in news commentaries and commercials on radio and TV and report on them in class. Make them aware of the effect of loaded words on the listener.

For enrichment, point out how loaded words can be used in a question.

Examples:

Do you still cheat on tests?
Was that the pencil you took?

Ask the pupils to identify the loaded words in the preceding questions. Discuss with them the implications and probable effects of these words. Have them listen for loaded questions in TV courtroom dramas. How does a lawyer sometimes use loaded questions?

Tell and Retell

AIM: *To understand the difference between hearing and listening.*

Ask two pupils to leave the room for a few minutes, and while they are absent relate a story, an incident, a tall tale, or a joke to the rest of the class.

Ask one of the pupils to return, and have a volunteer tell him or her the story in the full view and hearing of the class. Then ask the second child to re-enter the room, and have the first pupil tell him or her the story he or she just heard. Is the third rendition of the tale the same as the first? If not, how does it differ, and why? What does the activity tell about listening? Did everyone listen to the story? Does the speaker have anything to do with the listener? Repeat the activity from time to time in an effort to reduce the disparity.

To sustain interest, limit each session to one story and increase its length and complexity as the class becomes skilled in the activity.

What is the difference between hearing and listening? Elicit the conclusion that in order to listen effectively one must pay careful attention to the sounds.

The Sounds Around

AIM: *To understand the importance of listening.*

Take your class on a walk. When they have returned to the classroom, have them identify the various sounds they heard during the walk and list them on the chalkboard. Then discuss with them the nature and sources of the sounds around them. Does identification of the source of the sound have a significance?

Have the class keep a listening chart that records all the things they do during the school day that specifically involve listening, and the time devoted to listening during each activity. Have the pupils total the time periods daily and weekly, and calculate the percentage of time spent in listening per school day and week. The activity can be varied by having each pupil keep a chart of his own or her own listening experience during a given period of time and having a bulletin board chart representing a summary of the individual records.

Ask pupils to report on the sounds they heard during a specified period of time. Help the others to classify the sounds and have a class recorder keep a general record. At some point, discuss with the class the sounds they heard, the significance of each sound to their living experience, the frequency with which it is heard, and the kind of listening it requires. Why are some sounds more important than others? Under what conditions does the same sound become more important than usual? How are some sounds that we hear all the time made? What effect does sound have on our bodies? How are you awakened each morning? What sound level do family members prefer when listening to records, radio, or TV? What street sounds do you shut out? How are various alarm sounds made?

Listen to This!

AIM: *To identify and discriminate between sounds.*

Say aloud a pair of words which are either identical or simply similar in sound. Have the children stand up or raise their hands if the words they hear are the same, and remain seated or keep their hands down if the words they hear are different. For example: Are the words in each of the following pairs the same or different?

eat—meal
run—ran

boat—bone
late—soon

Help your pupils to discriminate aurally between voiced and unvoiced consonants by eliciting from them words that begin with a particular phoneme, such as /b/ or /p/, /v/ or /f/, /d/ or /t/. Appoint three monitors: one to choose among those who volunteer to answer; another to preclude duplication by keeping track of the words as they are suggested; and a third to keep score. Say aloud a phoneme. The child then names another phoneme, and so the game goes. Plus points are given for correct answers; minus points are given for duplicated or incorrect answers.

The activity can be adapted to improve the child's ability to discriminate between vowel sounds or between phonemes in other than initial positions.

Make up games which involve practice in the use of consonants, such as "I am thinking of a word that begins with 'l' and it is the name of an animal." (*lion, llama, lamb*)

Make a particular sound, such as *b*, or *s*, or *f* and then ask the pupils to listen for it at the beginning, at the end, or in the middle of a series of words. Reinforce their retention by having the class repeat in unison both the sound and the series of words that contain it.

Hot or Cold

AIM: *To help students recognize intonation patterns and their effects on meaning.*

Have the pupils locate a hidden object by listening to a rhythmic tom-tom beat which grows louder as the pupil approaches the object and softer as he draws away from it. After the exercise is completed, discuss with and demonstrate to the pupils the changes that can be made in intonation when the volume and/or tempo of beats is increased.

Divide the class into two teams. Using a musical instrument, play two different notes. (A piano works best, but a toy xylophone, a recorder, or a string instrument is satisfactory.) A child from one team is asked to tell whether the second note played was higher or lower in pitch then the first. A player from the other team responds next. The exercise continues until all members of each team have responded or a certain number of correct answers determines the winner.

Read a story in which the characters speak with decidedly different voices. Stop occasionally after a character has spoken and ask the pupils to identify the speaker. When the story is finished, repeat passages of dialogue out of context and have the children identify the character who is speaking.

In these activities and games, a player is said to be "hot" when he is close to guessing. Players who are far afield are said to be "cold."

—2—

VOCABULARY-BUILDING GAMES

Words, words, words—your pupils are bombarded by words coming out of their television sets, their teachers' mouths, and the printed page. Yet, many children speak with a limited vocabulary and are unfamiliar with many of the words that they manage to sound out phonetically.

What can you the teacher do about increasing your pupils' word power? How can you help your pupils use a variety of words in their daily speech and writing? From your own experience you have no doubt discovered that memorizing word lists is not the answer for every child. Poring over a dictionary is far from the best approach. What seems to work best is a "fun" approach. A painless, non-threatening approach to word acquisition is the only way for most pupils.

In this chapter we have assembled a variety of word games and activities that you can easily work into your daily routines. They have been used successfully by other teachers and none of them require much preparation. Perhaps their most practical feature is that pupils look forward to these activities as a break from more structured learning. Yet, these word energizers and games provide your pupils with concrete vocabulary building and insight into word relationships.

You will be able to see results after using these suggestions for just two weeks. Your pupils will recognize more words, speak with more clarity and preciseness, and write in a more mature manner. They will use the correct names of things in their own environment, describe actions of others more accurately, reinforce meanings, and form new words.

Try some of these brain-teasers as a "do-now" activity. Encourage your class to make up their own crossword puzzles using the suggestions found in this chapter.

What Kind?

AIM: *To teach certain basic adjectives.*

After viewing a filmstrip or seeing a class play, ask your pupils to name some of the people or objects they saw. Record on the chalkboard six or seven of the things they mention. A list such as the following may evolve: king, throne, castle, witch, lake, crowd.

Ask the children to describe each of these things with a single word. List four different responses for each thing seen in the play or filmstrip. For example:

old	rich	fat	mean	KING
tall	gold	heavy	wide	THRONE
stone	dark	big	gray	CASTLE
bad	black	evil	scary	WITCH
deep	large	pretty	blue	LAKE
noisy	loud	laughing	moving	CROWD

Compound Word Jigsaw

AIM: *To give young children experience in matching two small words to make new compound words.*

Start with four first-part words on cardboard:

some   tooth   saw   butter

Then make cards with:

body   brush   dust   fly

Hold ends of matching words together and cut edges in a wavy pattern. Pupils may then take all eight cards and form compound words. Correct matches will interlock as in a jigsaw puzzle. (See Figure 2-1.)

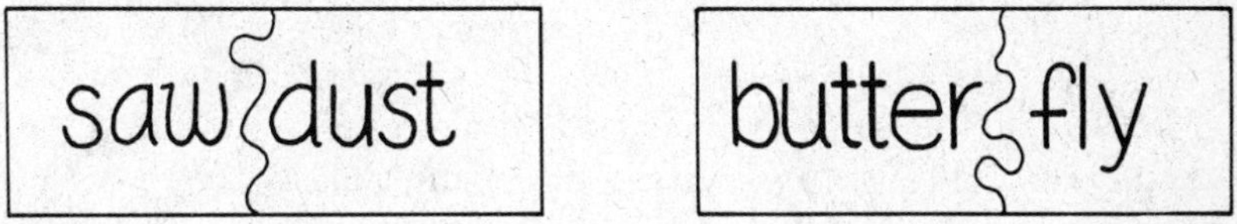

saw⟩dust   butter⟩fly

Figure 2-1

Action Word Game

AIM: *To introduce action words and review name words.*

Line up your class as if for a spelling bee with two even teams.

Prepare oaktag cards with simple action words lettered with a marking pen. Each child on one team is given a card, face down. He may not look at it until his turn comes to hold it up for all to see. His opposite number on the other team must now tell what object or utensil is used to perform the action on the card; e.g., if the card reads "cut," the child opposite must respond with an object or utensil like "scissors" or "knife." If he can't think of any answer or gives an incorrect one, he must sit. The child holding the card must now give the right answer, or sit.

At game's end, the team with the most remaining players wins'.

For younger children or for a slower class, you can omit the naming of the utensil and stick with just the action word. In this form the game resembles charades in the format of a spelling bee.

What's Happening?

AIM: *To get children to describe an action with a single word.*

Arrange a display (on chalkboard or side bulletin board) of pictures of animals or people actively doing something. Ask the class to describe what is going on in each picture. Record their correct responses on a single strip of oaktag. Tape or tack the correct action word near each picture. Remove the strips and have pupils match the action words with the appropriate pictures.

Help the pupils by writing some open sentences on the board, such as:

A duck is _____ in the pond.
The man is _____ a bike.
The monkey is _____ a ladder.
The girl is _____ a sandwich.

Word Relationships

AIM: *To help pupils see how words belong together.*

Put a sample on the board:

Bus is to people as truck is to things

Encourage your pupils to discuss the relationship that exists between a "bus" and "people." Ask, "Which carries which?" Then ask, "What does a truck carry?" Then have them fill in the following sentences:

1. Egg is to hen as seed is to _____
   (field   garden   flower)

2. Buzz is to bee as laugh is to _____
   (cry   noise   people)

3. Cat is to kitten as dog is to _____
   (puppy   animal   old)

4. Nose is to front as tail is to _____
   (animal   long   back)

5. Water is to clean as wood is to _____
   (paint   build   trees)

6. Pony is to animal as pine is to _____
   (tree   color   always)

On Stage

AIM: *To help pupils relate word meanings with actions in order to reinforce meanings.*

Hold up a picture of a child with a happy or sad face. Ask your pupils to describe the child's feelings. List the responses on the board. Call on pupils to come "on stage" and to act out the feelings listed, one at a time. You will probably get responses like:

gloomy	joyful
frowning	grinning
crying	jolly
laughing	laughing
weeping	smiling

Next, you list certain verbs on the board and have selected youngsters act them out "on stage." Try to group adjectives, verbs, nouns together.You need not label them as such. Your slower pupils will be able to see the relationships better if you work on just one part of speech at a time.

Word Sets

AIM: *To help pupils see words as related to similar words in meaning.*

The sets of words below are related to one another. Add a fourth word to each family or set.

Monday	Sunday	Friday	_____
March	April	July	_____
Circle	Square	Triangle	_____
Dog	Cat	Canary	_____
Ball	Sled	Jumprope	_____
Red	Blue	Green	_____
Apple	Banana	Pear	_____
Rose	Tulip	Zinnia	_____

Look Around

AIM: *To help children learn the names of things in their own environment.*

In this activity your pupils will be encouraged to look around their classroom to name things that they see that fit into certain broad categories.

Begin by asking them to name some things they see that are round. List these on the chalkboard under the title "Round." Then ask them to name items that are long, heavy, white, made of wood, etc. List all of these on the board or on a piece of oaktag. If you want to refer to these lists again, write them on a spiral tablet chart that you can refer to from time to time. With very young children or a slow class it would be wise to have these lists available for review and recall.

Capitalize on your pupils' imaginations by asking them to name things that are found in certain rooms of their homes: kitchen, bathroom, bedroom, basement, porch. Ask them to name parts of a car or their bicycle.

After these lists are made, have the children copy them into their notebooks. A meaningful homework assignment would be to find magazine pictures of some of these items.

As your class progresses, ask the pupils to alphabetize the items on a single list.

Have your pupils dictate a single sentence containing two or more of the words on a single list. Children love to see how many words they can cram into a single sentence. If this does not work, then you write on the board a sentence containing two or more words from a single group and ask the pupils to underline the words on the "Look Around" list in their notebook. When children become very familiar with some of these words, you may assign them as spelling words. Be sure to include the titles of the various categories as words for alphabetizing or spelling.

Letter Names

AIM: *To think of homonyms that sound like letters of the alphabet.*

Refer the class to the alphabet chart above the chalkboard.
Have pupils say each letter silently while they think of words that sound like the names of some of the letters.

Ask these questions:

What letter is a bird? (Jay = J)
What letter is a body of water? (Sea = C)
What letter is a green vegetable? (Pea = P)
What letter asks a question? (Why = Y)
What letter is an insect? (Bee = B)
What letter is something you drink? (Tea = T)

For older children you may ask:

What letter is a female animal? (Ewe = U)
What letter is a long line? (Queue = Q)
What letter is a girl's name? (Bea or Kay)
What letter is a pronoun? (You or I)
What letter is a signal? (Cue = Q)
What letter expresses debt? (Owe = O)
What letter is an organ of the body? (Eye = I)
What letter is a slang expression? (Gee = G)
What letter is a verb? (Are = R)
What letter is a prefix meaning "former"? (Ex = X)

This can be played as an exercise or warm-up for the whole class or as a competitive "word bee." If teams compete, you will need a timekeeper. Pupils love to ask these questions of one another in small-group situations also.

When asking the questions, be sure not to have the answers appear in strict alphabetical order since that will make it too easy for the average class.

Y-Grams

AIM: *To help children add a letter (y) to a small word and form a new word.*

Your children probably know something about anagrams or rearranging letters of nonsense syllables to form words. In Y-Grams you take off from that format by giving your pupils some simple words that they see all the time. They are then asked to form a new word by adding the letter "y" and rearranging the letters.

Place the word "are" on the chalkboard. Have one pupil come up and add the letter "y." He or she now has the four letters "a r e y." with a minute to think or a hint from the teacher, the pupil will then be able to write under it the word "year."

Here are fourteen other words that you can use. Next to each we have written the answer (which is a new word made by adding "y" and rearranging the letters):

sat	(stay)	raid	(dairy)
lap	(play)	real	(relay)
rat	(tray)	chat	(yacht)
see	(eyes)	dole	(yodel)
dear	(ready)	pear	(repay)
toad	(today)	near	(yearn)
dart	(tardy)	thou	(youth)

Variation: You can play MINUS Y on another occasion. Merely list the answer word and have the pupils remove the "y" and rearrange the letters. For example: S T A Y minus the Y becomes S A T.

Pictures in Words

AIM: *To help pupils visualize word meanings through creative lettering.*

Tell your pupils that they can doodle the letters of certain words to illustrate their meaning. They may want to use their vocabulary notebooks or spelling lists as a starting point. A few illustrations like these will trigger their own imaginations. One teacher placed a large piece of construction paper on a rear wall and encouraged children to use a flow ball pen to create a word picture during some free time. This gave the pupils an opportunity for "legal graffiti." (See Figure 2-2.)

Figure 2-2

Hand/Foot Word Builders

AIM: *To add to pupils' vocabularies words containing "hand" and "foot," and to give other meanings for these words.*

Begin the game by asking if anyone knows what a "handker-chief" is. The question will bring an almost universal response. The teacher then explains what a kerchief is, and the picture of a handker-chief emerges.

Ask questions such as:

1. What has "hand" in it, and is used by a policeman?
   (*handcuffs*)
2. What has "hand" in it and might be seen on a piece of paper?
   (*handwriting*)
3. Can you think of the name of a game that has the word "foot" in it?
   (*football*)
4. Jane's sweater was made at home. We can say it is _____.
   (*handmade*)
5. At the beach you leave _____ in the wet sand.
   (*footprints*)
6. What is the name of a small bridge not big enough for cars?
   (*footbridge*)
7. In the haunted house we heard _____ on the stairs.
   (*footsteps*)
8. The clock has a minute _____.
   (*hand*)
9. The marigold has grown a _____ since last month.
   (*foot*)
10. The captain announced, "All _____ on deck."
    (*hands*)
11. Dad asked, "Please give me a _____ with the trash."
    (*hand*)
12. The carpet was torn at the _____ of the stairs.
    (*foot*)

Newspaper Search

AIM: *To strengthen vocabulary skills by searching for words on a single topic.*

Bring to class two or three copies of a daily newspaper. Take the paper apart and give each child one or two sheets. The object of the activity is for a child to underline in red all the words he can find on a given subject. As you hand out each sheet, write a subject in marking pen at the top of the page. For example: *Time*. The youngsters would then underline such words as: day, hour, year, month. Suitable topics include transportation, foods, health, geography, communication, games.

> *Hint*: When you assign a sheet or sheets to a child, scan the page to see which topic would be suitable. If you are handing him the sports page, don't ask him to look for "food" words.

Tugboat

AIM: *To teach pupils to form compound words from familiar component words.*

Make two lists on the board or on an old window shade. Since this game can be played many times a permanent listing will be worth the effort. The length of each list will vary with the class. Divide the class into two teams. Tell the class that Column A words are tugboats, and Column B words are cargoes that need to be pulled into shore—but only certain tugboats can pull certain cargoes.

Line two teams up against the side walls. Have the first player from Team One come up to the board and attach a piece of yarn (with tape at each end) from one of the tugboats to one of the cargoes. In order to earn a point he must use the new word he has made in a sentence. Then have the first player from the second team do the same.

Add to the excitement by having one list longer than the other. Assign one pupil as timekeeper.

Scrambled Eggs

AIM: *To teach sight vocabulary words appropriate to holidays.*

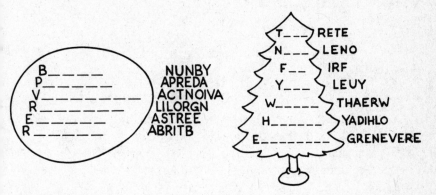

Figure 2-3

At different times of the year you want your pupils to be able to identify certain basic sight vocabulary words that are appropriate to that time of the year. These words may not be part of the basal reader, yet your pupils will see them on greeting cards and elsewhere. They may also want to use them in their written expression. After writing them on the chalkboard or on some experience chart, you may want to check to see if your pupils have mastered them. A fun way to do this is by preparing a spirit duplicating master with a large drawing appropriate to the holiday, such as an Easter egg. On it you letter the initial sound of these key words and sufficient blanks for the remaining letters. Below, or alongside, you scramble *all* the letters of the word. For Christmas we have drawn a tree outline with some suggested words.

For other occasions we suggest:

Election Day—a ballot box with these words: vote, poll, victory, winner, count.
Thanksgiving Day—a turkey, with table, bird, trimmings, turkey, Pilgrims, November.

Columbus Day—A ship, with Nina, Pinta, Santa Maria, ocean, Spain, explore.

Vocabulary Golf

AIM: *To provide pupils with practice in using a dictionary to find synonyms.*

On the chalkboard list 18 words representing the 18 holes of golf. Players use their dictionaries to find a synonym for each word. They are encouraged to find the *shortest* synonym possible. Each letter of the synonym counts as one point. For some words the teacher can indicate "par" in parentheses next to the word. The player with the lowest score wins. Score 18 points for any word for which a player cannot find a synonym.

A variation can be played, in which long words are sought and the highest score wins.

Pupils can call different words "sand traps," or use other golf terms.

Putting It Together

AIM: *To acquaint pupils with combining forms, such as bio-, auto-, geo-, tele-, photo-, and -gram, -graph, -graphy, and -phone.*

Show how combining forms can be joined with other words or each other to make new words. After pupils use their dictionaries to get the meaning of these nine forms, quiz them with these nine fill-ins.

1. A person's signature: _____.
2. Making pictures with light: _____.
3. The written story of a person's life: _____.
4. A written message from far away: _____.
5. Something made by light: _____.
6. A person's life story written by that person: _____.
7. Something used to send sound over a long distance: _____.
8. A description of the earth: _____.
9. Sending messages over a long distance: _____.

Initial Soundings

AIM: *To build words upon an initial syllable. (This vocabulary builder calls for a good ear and a good memory.)*

The teacher writes a syllable on the board. At first it is best to use syllables that are words, such as "pen" "cat" or "man." Later on, you can use syllables like: cur- mis-, etc.

The first player begins by asking a question for which the answer begins with this initial sound. For example:

"What sort of pen is a fine?"   *(penalty)*

The pupil who answers this correctly asks a question of his or her own, such as:

"What sort of pen is a baseball flag?"   (pennant)

Other questions for "pen" might include:

"What kind of pen is atop a tall building?"   (penthouse)
"What sort of pen describes thought?"   (pensive)
"What kind of pen can you find on a clock?"   (pendulum)
"What kind of pen is the state of Florida?"   (peninsula)

For the syllable "cat" you might have questions that can be answered with these words: caterpillar, catalogue, catnip, cataract, catastrophe, category, catalyst, etc.

By all means, accept homonyms. If the initial sound is "new," you can also accept neutral, numeral, pneumonia, etc.

A good way to proceed is to go up and down each row. The next player must guess what the word is. If he does so, he then thinks of a word beginning with the syllable and asks the next player a question. Players drop out if they are unable to guess the word or think of a new word beginning with the same sound. If no one can think of another word with that syllable, the stumped player begins with a new syllable of his own choosing.

Word Pyramid

AIM: *To form words using only certain letters.*

Using the letters S M R T E S A form seven different words. Draw a pyramid like the one in Figure 2-4 on a piece of paper. Put only one letter in each building block.

Figure 2-4

Start with a one-letter word at the top. Next, write in a two-letter word, using the letter in the top block plus one other. Beneath this put in a three-letter word, using the two-letter word plus one additional letter. Keep this up until you use up all seven letters.

You will be amazed to find out that there are several different answers to this puzzle. Here are some of many correct combinations:

```
        A                       A
       A S                     A T
      S A T                   R A T
      S E A T                 R A T E
     T E A M S               S T A R E
    S T R E A M             M A S T E R
   M A S T E R S           S T R E A M S
```

Have pupils construct word pyramids of their own, using only five or six building blocks as the base word. You can assist them by suggesting that they include *A* and *E* as the vowels and an *S* as one of the consonants. After some practice, your pupils will develop an understanding of word families—and of the game of anagrams.

Crossword Puzzle Construction

AIM: *To assist pupils in making their own crossword puzzles.*

Did you ever wonder how you could construct your own crossword puzzle without spending hours doing it? The simplest way to start is to play Scrabble with a friend or by yourself. Then transpose the "board" with all the words onto paper. You can shade in the spaces or cut out around the puzzle to make an unusual shape. Number the spaces to match the list of definitions. Write "across" and "down" columns of definitions.

Make it easy for yourself by writing all the words in caps. Also, if you end up with two letters that don't make sense, create some abbreviations: define CG as coast guard or MM as initials of Mary Murray (a pupil in your class).

For pupils in the lower grades, make the definitions "clue lines" for fill-ins. For example, "Mary had a little _____."

After you have done some general puzzles, try some on a particular topic. For instance, do one on ecology, or this week's spelling words. Try one using contractions or abbreviations.

If you have bilingual children, try a puzzle with the words in English (simple nouns and verbs) and the definitions in Spanish.

Do one in numbers. The definitions are problems and their answers are the puzzle answers.

How about a social studies puzzle? Try one with proper names in American history or places settled by early explorers.

Try one where all the words are four letters or less.

Theme puzzles are fun: holidays, hobbies, sports, names of pupils in the class.

Hints:

1. Use words with double letters or similar letters in the middle, at the beginning or the end, allowing for elasticity in spacing to get the best interlocking.
2. Try to conserve spaces between words.
3. Don't miss numbering squares that begin in the middle of other words. For very young children, use pictures as cues. The simple line drawings of phonics books are great.
4. Subject puzzles help pupils think about the topic as well as the individual words.

Foreign Accent

AIM: *To give pupils an awareness that English includes many words from other languages. Give this quiz which highlights some of the Spanish words that have enriched our language.*

Finish these sentences by putting in one of these Spanish words:

adobe	taco
cargo	palomino
chile	rodeo
corral	siesta
Florida	patio
mosquito	pronto

1. I rode a _____ at the dude ranch.
2. The ranch hands herded the cattle into the _____.
3. My brother had a big bowl of _____ for supper.
4. The ship carried a _____ of gold from Africa.
5. It was too hot to work, so Pedro took a little _____ right after lunch.
6. Tex won the steer-roping contest in the _____ last week.
7. We're going to _____ for our vacation.
8. The boss shouted, "Get it ready _____."
9. They put an _____ wall aound the patio.
10. Last night, a _____ bit me while I slept.
11. The thin, fried _____ was crisp.
12. After supper, I sat on the _____.

Compound Interest

AIM: *To provide practice in forming compound words.*

Divide the class into five teams or rows. Each team has the first part of several compound words, e.g., Team I may have "back." The teacher will call a list of words one at a time. Each team listens to see if the word called can be joined to their first part word. E.g., when the teacher calls out "bone" or "stroke," Team I ("back") will note them because together they form compound words "backbone" and "backstroke."

When the teacher calls "mate" or "yard," the team called "ship" will note the compound words formed. The first team to list six compound words wins.

Here are some good team words (first part words):

back   ship   hand   thunder   land

Each of these second part words can be joined to one of the above. Mix them up from game to game to insure a different winner.

lord	cuff	pack	board	shower
bird	stage	stamp	slide	shake
ache	mark	load	storm	bolt
owner	locked	bone	ground	made
scape	mate	writing	stroke	book
shape	clap	struck	wreck	yard

Trick or Treat

AIM: *To form several words from a single root word* (trick *or* treat).

Around Halloween, or at any other time, write the word "trick" on the board. Ask pupils to make compound words or other words that begin with the five letters: trick/treat. Write the following open sentences on the board. (The correct response appears on the right.) For a slow class, use the answers as a matching game. Of course, dozens of other words can be used instead of "trick" or "treat."

1. There is a _____ from the faucet.   trickle
2. The test had many _____ questions.   tricky
3. Her illness was easily _____.   treated
4. A magician knows many _____.   tricks

5. He went to the clinic for _____.   treatment
6. Jim _____ John to a movie.   treated
7. The two countries signed a _____.   treaty
8. A cheater or magician can be called a _____.   trickster

Find the Relative

AIM: *To help pupils see word parts in other words.*

Tell the class you are going to write some short sentences on the board. They are to find family members (relatives) hidden among the words of the sentence. Give them this example:

I like the soFA THERe.

(The answer is underlined for you.)

1. She is so slim, others should diet.

(Capitalize **MOTHER** if a second sample is needed.)

2. An honest racer will run clean.

3. Why did the tree limb rot here?

(We have underlined the answers for the reader's convenience.)

4. That dress is terrific.

5. He made stucco using cement.

6. The picture's on the desk.

7. The genie certainly looked tall.

(Find the word "niece.")

8. The music was grand so now play another record.

(You're on your own with this one.)

—3—

READING-SKILL BUILDERS

The first of the three R's is the skill you teach most of the school day in various forms. Do some of your pupils groan when you hand out the phonics books, basal readers, workbooks, or other reading materials? As an experienced teacher you know that children would rather be playing a game. This chapter will give you an arsenal of reading games, brain teasers, puzzles and other activities that spark your pupils' interest while giving them instruction and practice in reading skills.

Some are card games with a reading twist, some are familiar children's games with an added reading dimension. Practice in sounding out long and short vowels can now be given painlessly. Ideas for reading enjoyment abound.

These snappy reading activities will help you introduce new material as well as cloak needed practice and reinforcement in a more palatable format.

Down and Out

AIM: *To practice identifying and pronouncing sight words.*

Children love card games, and this one is based on an old favorite, Down and Out.

The object of this card game is for a player to be the first to discard all cards from his hand. He or she does this by matching sight words and reading them aloud. If he or she cannot read them aloud correctly the cards must be put back into the hand.

Begin by dividing the class into groups of four players. Any extra pupils can serve as auditors. Auditors walk around the room checking to see that the rules of the game are followed and that the words are pronounced correctly.

The teacher gives each group of four a deck of sight word cards (51 cards in the deck: 25 sight words, two cards for each word; plus one card labeled "OUT").

Beginning with the pupil on the dealer's left, each player takes turns drawing one card from the player on his right. As pairs are formed, the words are pronounced and the pair is placed on the table.

The first pupil to use all the cards in his hand is the winner and the new dealer. One person will be left with the card marked "OUT."

Blend Bingo

AIM: *To introduce consonant blends dr, fl, fr.*

Tell your pupils:

dr is the sound you hear at the beginning of *dry*.
fl is the sound you hear at the beginning of *fly*.
fr is the sound you hear at the beginning of *fry*.

Give examples of these words in sentences. Ask pupil volunteers to name other words that begin with these blends.

Review previously learned blends such as bl, br, cl, cr, th, wh, sh, ch.

Prepare two Bingo cards on the chalkboard with 25 squares in each (5 rows × 5 columns). You may want to make the middle square a FREE box.

Insert the various blends learned, including the three new ones: dr, fl, fr. Be sure each of the two Bingo cards is different.

The point of this team game is for each team to mark five boxes in a row on its Bingo blend card by identifying consonant blends.

Divide the class into two teams. Each team selects one pupil to write on the card the marks which the team decides should be made. Colored chalk is good for this.

The teacher mixes word cards in a box. Have one pupil in the class serve as caller. He or she selects a card at random and reads the word aloud.

When the word is read, each team decides how the word begins and marks the corresponding word on the card. Only one box on the chalkboard card can be marked for each word. The team-selected pupil-marker uses his or her own judgment as to which blend to mark with the colored chalk.

The first team to mark five consecutive boxes in any direction is the winner.

Spell-and-Read

AIM: *To make as many four-letter long-vowel words as possible.*

For this game you will need to make a set of five dice for each group of three or four pupils. You may use dice that have other numbers or letters on them and cover them over with masking tape; you may use sponge rubber cubes with squares of tape on each surface; or you may make cubes out of cardboard as illustrated, in Figure 3-1.

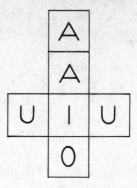

Figure 3-1

These are the letters to go on each die (use capital letters to avoid confusion):

A	A	I	O	U	U
T	T	M	M	N	N
C	C	T	T	M	M
T	T	N	N	P	P
E	E	E	E	E	E

Using a paper cup or other canister, the first player shakes and rolls the dice. He or she makes as many four-letter words as possible. Proper names do not count.

If the player cannot form any words, and if the other players agree that there are no possible words, he may roll the dice one more time. If the other players have found words, the original player loses his turn. The pupil on the player's right goes next, and so on.

To score: a player wins 100 points for each four-letter word that is formed. Encourage your class to use the dictionary if pupils are not sure of a word.

Marathon

AIM: *To reinforce sight words.*

This is a quickie activity game. On 20 to 25 separate pieces of construction paper, attach different pictures of objects cut from a magazine. For each picture make a card with the word or words that describe the object. Place several pictures around the classroom or on the bulletin board. Put their corresponding cards in a box nearby. Divide your class into teams and let each player draw one card. A player must place his card under the correct picture. If he or she places it under the wrong picture, the card goes back into the box. The team with the most cards correct wins.

Long "A" Quiz

AIM: *To quiz the class on their ability to pick out long "a."*

List between 15 and 20 words on the board. Include these correct answer words as well as words with a short "a" sound.

For the teacher's convenience we are putting the correct answer word in parenthesis after each question. Tell the class that you are going to think of a word on the list. If they listen to the clue you give them, they will be able to track down the word you are thinking of. They are to raise their hands when they know the answer. Here are the clues:

1. How old something is.   (*age*)
2. There are fifty in the United States.   (*states*)
3. Name for a young Indian man.   (*brave*)
4. A boy and a girl go out on a _____.   (*date*)
5. A story.   (*tale*)
6. To do or produce something.   (*make*)
7. You find these in a book.   (*pages*)
8. You need an oven to do this.   (*bake*)
9. A name for circles, squares, and triangles.   (*shapes*)
10. The door in a fence.   (*gate*)
11. A kind of dessert.   (*cake*)
12. A car must stay in _____.   (*lane*)

"Wrong One"

AIM: *To use a learning center puzzle that young children can walk up to and do; this one reviews blends.*

How to make:

Use 10 to 12 large manila envelopes. Cut them as seen in Figure 3-2.
Cut two one-inch circles for train wheels.
Cut a strip of oaktag and print a blend on it.
Cut out pictures that are approximately 2 × 4.
Paste a picture that corresponds to the blend on each card.
Laminate each mounted picture with clear adhesive paper, such as Con-Tact. This will enable pupils to mark pictures with a crayon that can be rubbed off later.

How to use:

Players look at the picture cards in the cars of the train. Players decide which one doesn't belong and pull that one out. The one that doesn't belong is marked with an X for immediate reinforcement.

Try to change the picture cards and letter cards every day. Place a record chart near the center. Each day when the child completes a task he or she can place a star next to his or her name.

Figure 3-2

Vowel Math Code

AIM: *To use a code format to help pupils review vowel sounds.*

Using the following code, put the correct number on the line under each word. If you do this correctly, your math problem will be correct as well.

Code: Rhymes with role = 1   came = 6
                        nine = 2   meal = 7
                        Sue = 3   coat = 8
                        lake = 4   fire = 9
                        feet = 5   June = 0

wire	− tame	= clue		fine	+ take	+ glue	= hire
____	− ____	= ____		____	+ ____	+ ____	= ____
deal	+ hole	= goat		pole	+ note	+ tune	= wire
____	+ ____	= ____		____	+ ____	+ ____	= ____
boat	− beet	= flu_		tire	− feel	− line	= dune
____	− ____	= ____		____	− ____	− ____	= ____
same	− bake	= wine					
____	− ____	= ____					

Sound Off

AIM: *To reinforce sound-symbol association skills and teach vowel discrimination.*

Draw a path containing about 60 spaces, write a vowel on each space, and mount the path on cardboard. Make up a set of cards of two colors of construction paper, putting pictures of objects representing short vowels on one color and long vowel objects on the second color. Use poker chips for game pieces.

Start by studying the picture cards representing short vowels. When they have been mastered, go on to the long vowel cards. Then mix all the cards together.

Each player draws a card, says the word pictured on it, and advances his poker chip to the next space on the path containing the correct vowel. For example, if the picture card shows a bed, the chip must be placed on the next "e" space.

Reading Directions (Code Book)

AIM: *To give pupils practice in following directions; using codes.*

Pupils love to write in code. This brain teaser involves devising a code with directions for decoding plus a coded message to practice on.

The best way for the teacher to provide everyone with the experience is to run off a rexographed master. Our sample is included for your use. Before you launch your class you may want to talk about codes and have your pupils read about them. Emphasize that as "secret agents" they must carefully study the directions for decoding and write them down so that a "fellow agent" or partner will be able to decode the message.

You have no doubt found through the years that pupils do not take time to read directions to the end. This brain teaser will erase that bad practice and will also encourage pupils to check their work.

Encourage your class to make up codes that follow some pattern; i.e., work backwards in the alphabet, or alternate letters beginning with "g", etc. Here is our CODE BOOK Worksheet; every pupil gets a copy.

CODE BOOK

The secret code devised below was the product of the superior intelligence of FBI agent _____ also known as: _____.

Regular
Alphabet: A B C D E F G H I J K L M N O P Q R S T U V W X Y Z

Code
Alphabet: _____
Directions to Fellow Agent:

Sample Message:

Decoded Message:

Signature of Fellow Agent:

Fish-a-Word

AIM: *To improve sight vocabulary.*

The object of this game is for players to accumulate as many pairs of cards as possible by matching words learned in the previous reading lesson. Words printed on oaktag will do.

Have students get into groups of two, three, or four. Tell them that this game is the same as "Fish" except that they will be playing with words they have learned in their reading lesson.

The dealer deals four cards to each pupil and places the rest of the pack face down on the table. The first player asks another player if he has a certain word which matches one in his own hand. If the child asked has the card, he must give it up.

When a player succeeds in making a pair, he lays the pair on the table and gets another turn. If the player asked does not have the card, he tells the one who asked to "fish." To fish means to take one card from the pack.

If the card the player draws is the one he was asking for, he continues to play. If not, his turn ends. Any time a pupil runs out of cards, he may take three from the pack. Hands should never include more than six cards at a time. Extra cards should be discarded to the bottom of the stack. Play continues until the pack is used up.

If a pupil does not know a word in his hand, he may ask for help, but must then give up his turn and wait until the next turn to ask for his card. This is risky, as someone else might need that card and might ask for it first. The player with the most pairs at the end of the game wins.

Word-Maker

AIM: *To stimulate children to form their own words.*

Most words in our language are made up of a consonant sound, a vowel sound, and another consonant sound. To these are added suffixes to form new words.

Here is a brain teaser that your pupils will enjoy while they learn to manipulate letters to make words. All you need for this activity is our list of consonants, vowels, and suffixes, and a chalkboard.

Begin by drawing four large squares alongside one another on the board. These will represent the four elements of the words that the pupils must guess. Notice we did not say four "letters" because some sounds have two or three letters. As an aid you may label these four squares: c, v, c, s. This will help the class understand that the first sound will always be a consonant, the second a vowel, the third a consonant, and the fourth a suffix.

Here are our lists that will save you a lot of work:

Initial Consonant Sounds				Vowel Sounds			Final Consonant Sounds				Suffixes	
b	g	qu	str	a	al	oi	b	ik	p	sh	ed	able
bl	gl	r	sw	e	au	ou	c	ll	pt	sk	er	s
br	gr	s	t	i	ea	oo	ch	lp	r	sp	est	es
c	h	sc	th	o	ee	ui	ck	lt	rb	ss	ful	less
ch	j	scr	tr	u	ie	y	d	m	rd	st	ing	
cl	k	sh	tw	y	oa		f	mb	rk	t	ly	
cr	l	sl	v				ff	mp	rl	th		
d	m	sm	w				ft	n	rm	tt		
dr	n	sn	wh				g	nd	rn	w		
f	p	sp	y				l	ng	rp	y		
fl	pl	spr	z				lb	nk	rt			
fr	pr	st					ld	nt	s			

Now, you as the teacher need only select one consonant from our first list to put in the first square, then one vowel sound from our second column for the second square, and so on for squares three and four. After you have done a few familiar words this way, the fun begins. You now think of a word and omit the sounds for one or two squares. Your pupils put their thinking caps on to come up with the word you are thinking about. For example: gr ou_____less (groundless).

Find the Rhyme

AIM: *To practice pairing rhyming words.*

This is a card game similar to "Concentration." Before you actually play have the pupils prepare the cards needed. Hand out sets of 32 3 × 5 index cards to half the pupils. These pupils each choose one partner. Each pair of partners receives 32 cards, or 16 cards for each player. One of the short "e" words taken from your chalkboard list is written on each card. You may, of course, use another long or short vowel sound.

Write two lists of words on the board, draw a line down the center, and have the first player in each pair copy the words on one side of the line, and the second player all the rest. Tell them to write carefully with large letters so the cards will be easy to read.

After all the pairs of players have completed their decks, tell them to shuffle the cards face down, then spread them out on two desks pushed together, or the floor, or any surface large enough to hold all the cards. To begin the game, the first partner turns two of the cards face up. If they rhyme with each other, he picks them up and puts them in his pile, then may try again with two other cards. If the second two don't rhyme, he turns them back face down in the same space. Then the second player turns up two other cards, and tries to get a rhyming pair. The first card he or she turns up must be a different card from the two turned up by his partner, but if that first card makes a rhyme with one of the two his partner just turned over, he may pick up the rhyming card as his second to make a pair. If, that is, he or she remembers where it was. Each time any partner makes a pair, he gets another try.

The game goes on with the partners alternating turns until the entire deck has been paired. Then the partners count up their cards, and the one with the most cards wins.

Bookmaking

AIM: *To help children write their own books.*

Many pupils regard the object we call a book with fear and loathing. A successful reversal of this feeling can be accomplished when pupils create their own books. Let them dictate, write, print, staple, illustrate, and share their very own books. These then become objects of pride and affection. These books must be reflections of their experiences, their words, their ideas, and their format.

The impact of handmade books brings pupils into positive contact with books and reading. Here are a few themes for bookmaking that have worked well in other schools:

1. *A pet journal.* Compile a log of the growth and development of a classroom pet. Include personal observations and feelings about the pet.

2. *A how-to book.* Write the various steps followed in the making of a handcrafted article or the assembling and care of a bike or moped.

3. *Collection of jokes.* Pupils love to put together jokes and one-liners that tickle their fancies. They will re-read these books more than many others.

4. *Rewrite fiction.* Read to the class a well-known piece of literature such as an O. Henry short story. Then ask the pupils to retell the tale in their own words. Rewrite the story, using their vocabulary and manner of speech.

5. *Yellow pages.* Pupils have strong feelings about local vendors and community services. Encourage them to write a classified directory similar to the telephone company's yellow pages. They can list their favorite stores and eateries. Be sure that they do not include any negative comments about shops not included or recommended.

CB Language

AIM: *To enrich pupils' language while furthering an appreciation of social studies.*

One of the most exciting trends in recent years has been the growth of citizen's band radios or CB. Your pupils are aware of it and are picking up a whole new language. Why not capitalize on it by expanding some of these language experiences in the classroom? There are several quizzes and energizers that have worked well, such as these:

1. Prepare your class' own CB dictionary.
2. Quiz pupils on common CB terms.
3. Compose and decode CB messages on the chalkboard.
4. Improvise CB dialogue in telling a story.
5. Write letters to CB operators.
6. Bring in advertisements for CB equipment and comparison shop as a class.
7. Invite a CB operator-parent to visit class and tell of some exciting CB experience.
8. Locate these CB cities on the map: Big Apple, Motown, Lost Wages, Angel City, Chi Town, Jazz City.
9. Make available for perusal CB magazines and dictionaries.
10. Investigate kinds of trucks such as cold rig, muck truck, ten-wheeler, soda fountain.

Cloze Quiz

AIM: *To develop reading comprehension skills (context).*

In this quiz activity pupils are presented with reading material in which one or more words are omitted from each sentence. The pupil is confronted with the task of restoring the missing words in order to get the full meaning. To do so, the pupil must rely on certain clues. The context or sense of the sentence provides the meaning. Through this experience the pupils will also intuitively grasp the concept of *noun* and *verb*. For example:

Shirley likes to eat _____ for lunch.
Jack _____ quickly down the street.

In the first sentence it is obviously a "naming word" that is missing. In the second, it is an "action word." As a variation, a graphic clue may be supplied by giving the initial letter of the missing word in some of the exercise sentences.

Later, you can go beyond the one-sentence training exercises that are needed at first. Here you use any reading selection of 250 to 300 words, so long as the selection is at the individual's reading level. Usually the first and last sentences are left intact. After that, every 10th or 15th word is deleted. If this is material that can be marked on, the deletion can be made by marking over the words to be deleted with a felt tip marker. This will provide the added clue of word length.

The pupil is then given the selection to read and must determine what the missing words are by using the context. When cloze procedure is used for teaching purposes, synonyms for the missing words are always acceptable, whereas testing requires exact replacement words.

The level of the reading material, the number of words omitted, and the type of words omitted will determine the difficulty and the appropriateness of the task for the grade and level of reading ability.

Wigwams

AIM: *To reinforce long and short vowel sounds.*

This is a seat game that two pupils can play independently from the rest of the glass. You can divide the class into pairs and everyone can play. It is essentially a variation of the game "Hangman," which many pupils may know.

One player thinks of a word with a vowel in it. He or she must announce the vowel being used. He or she then draws on a sheet of paper the correct number of blanks for the word in mind. One blank for each letter is drawn. His or her partner then begins guessing the word, letter by letter. For each incorrect guess, the first player draws one part of a wigwam. The parts of a wigwam are drawn on the board for pupils to copy (Figure 3-3).

After the first player has drawn two wigwams the player trying to guess the word loses. He or she must now think of a word himself or herself. If the player guesses the word correctly before two wigwams are drawn, then he or she must tell whether the word has a long or short vowel sound. If he or she can't do that, neither player wins. It is a tie. If the sound is correctly described, a point is won.

For slow classes you may want to make a large chart with many suggested words under long and short vowel sound columns, from which the children can select one.

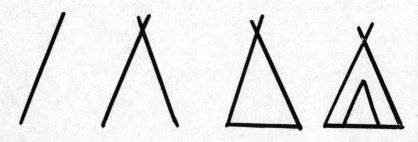

Figure 3-3

Puzzle—N

AIM: *To introduce pupils to the joys of crossword puzzles.*

Some youngsters are afraid to begin crossword puzzles because of an earlier frustration or difficulty. A good way to overcome this and also teach an initial consonant sound is to make up a puzzle where all the definitions begin with the same letter. Here we have chosen the letter "n." All the words in this puzzle begin with the consonant "n." For a slow group you may want to list the definitions or "answers" in random order on the board and have children refer to them in filling in the appropriate squares. See Figure 3-4.

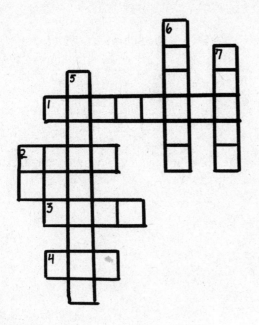

Figure 3-4

ACROSS	Definitions
1. Someone who lives near you.	neighbor
2. You use this to smell.	nose
3. What you are called.	name
4. Not old.	new

DOWN	
2. Not yes.	no
5. Where you read the news.	newspaper
6. You count with this.	number
7. Not south.	north

—4—

FUN WITH MATHEMATICS

Many parents excuse their youngster's poor performance in mathematics by saying, "He (or she) has always had a mental block when it comes to math." Such a mental block, if it does indeed exist, is undoubtedly caused by the feeling that math is too "different," too difficult, or too dull. The aura of mystery, or ennui, that surrounds numbers for many pupils can be quickly dispelled if you have at your fingertips an arsenal of puzzles, games, and energizers.

This chapter will supply you with just that. It will provide a bagful of board games, "do-now" activities, and brain teasers that will get your pupils to "think mathematically." When such activities are sandwiched in between other lessons, your pupils won't even realize that they are "doing math."

One of the most onerous tasks is to get pupils to learn their number facts, or tables. This chapter will show you a fresh approach. There are also techniques for teaching the telling of time, estimating answers, understanding fractions, Roman numerals, graphs, and mental arithmetic.

There are many times during the day when you have preparations to make and you would welcome some quiet and meaningful seatwork for your pupils. We call our suggestions for such an activity "do-now." All you have to do is write our "do-now" on the chalkboard and your pupils will dive right in. "Back to Zero" and

"Magic Squares" are two examples of math "do-nows" that you will find in this chapter.

More or Less

AIM: *To provide practice in responding to the language of math problems when terms like "more" or "less," "greater" or "smaller" are used.*

This game of chance also provides considerable practice in handling large numbers. All you need are two blank dice cubes. Label the faces of one cube with the four terms mentioned above. Label the other cube with the numbers 10, 100, and 1000. Start each player with a set number. This can be a familiar number such as your classroom (114) or the current year or a number at random (1354). The first player rolls the dice and figures the 10, 100, or 1000 "more" or "less," "greater" or "smaller." Pupils do the computation mentally but keep their score on a piece of paper. The winner is the pupil with the highest score after ten rolls.

The game is all chance, but math skills get a workout painlessly.

Back to Zero

AIM: *To provide subtraction practice.*

Take any number. *Example:* 3549.

Find the difference between each adjacent digit, and between the two end digits. Continue the process until you end up with all zeros.

Example (Figure 4-1):

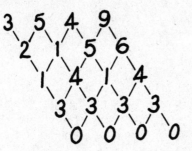

Figure 4-1

Discover-a-Fact

AIM: *To reinforce multiplication facts using a picture puzzle approach.*

Find a large picture and mount it on a piece of cardboard measuring 11″ × 12″. Line this mounted picture off in boxes. Each box should be about 1½″ by 2″. Now cut up the picture. You will have 42 pieces. On a piece of tagboard that also measures 11″ × 12″ rule boxes that will approximate your original picture. Arrange the pieces on blank tagboard. One at a time, lift the picture pieces and on each one write a multiplication fact question, such as 4 × 9 = _____. In the corresponding blank box of the tagboard, write the answer (36). Do this for all the pieces of the picture, with the answers in the.corresponding space on the tagboard.

Your pupils select one card at a time and place it picture side up on the correct answer on the "Discover-a-Fact Picture Card." Continue until the picture is completed.

Hint: Avoid as far as possible number facts that have the same answer as another fact, such as 4 × 4 and 2 × 8. You may find you have to use a few of these, depending on the number of squares in your picture.

How Square Are You?

AIM: *To review simple linear measure and squares and rectangles.*

      Draw three shapes on the chalk board: square, wide rectangle, and tall rectangle. Elicit a discussion of the differences between the two rectangles. Divide the class into pairs. Give each pair a cloth tape measure (either Metric or English). Have members of each pair measure both the arm spread and the height of their partner. Have them record this data in their notebook. Next, they decide whether the data produces a square, a wide rectangle, or a tall rectangle.

      Enrichment: For more advanced pupils, have them make a bar graph with bars for each shape. Then ask questions like: "How many more wide rectangles than squares were there?"

Sense Quiz

AIM: *To help young pupils estimate answers. This will help them avoid ridiculous answers when they compute solutions to verbal problems.*

      Write a simple paragraph on the chalkboard:

      Ramon is 9 years old. He lives in a big city.

      Hand out a ditto sheet with twelve questions that ask something about Ramon. Instruct pupils to underline the best answer.

      1. How many blocks does Ramon walk to school?

                       3   30   300

2. How many books does he carry to school?
   4   40   400

3. How many cents does he spend for lunch?
   5   50   500

4. How many children are in his room at school?
   3   30   300

5. How many children are in the whole class?
   7   70   700

6. How old is Ramon's younger sister?
   6   60   600

7. How old is his older brother?
   1   10   100

8. How many dogs does Ramon have?
   2   20   200

9. How many eggs does Ramon eat for breakfast?
   1   10   100

10. How many boys come to his house to play?
    5   50   500

11. How many hours a day does he spend sleeping?
    9   90   900

12. How many minutes does Ramon spend in school each day?
    3   30   300

Telling Time

AIM: *To help pupils learn to tell time.*

Digital Time Game

The omnipresent digital clocks and watches can help your pupils learn to tell time on the conventional clock face. The digital clock shows time passing in numbered sequences, using the familiar left-to-right sequence. Changes in time are shown by the simple

addition of ones to the minute and hour digits. After 3:59 the entire
reading line visibly changes to four o'clock and it is no longer an
abstraction.

Set up your digital clock underneath your circular clock with
the time synchronized, to help children figure out the circular time
machine.

Have pupils take turns calling out the correct time as the hands
of the clock move around the dial. Do this six or seven times during
the day, taking the pupils by surprise. Give points to the row in which
the pupil who gives the correct response sits.

Pupil Clock Face

Find two yardsticks to use for the hands of the clock. Cut one
shorter for use as the hour hand. Make the numerals one through 12 to
be pinned on the shirts of 12 children. Arrange 12 children in a circle
with numerals in the order found on a clock. Place the yardsticks in
the center of the circle, representing the hands on the clock.

The rest of the class members stand in line and take turns
showing the time on the "Pupil Clock Face" as called by the teacher.
If the child correctly shows the time, he chooses one of the numerals
and changes places with that person. That child goes to the end of the
line and takes his turn at the game.

Clock Arithmetic

AIM: *To provide practice in adding and subtracting numerals up
to 12.*

Draw a large circle on the chalk board. Have different pupils
come up to the board to place the 12 numerals as they appear on a
clock.

The teacher writes a number in the center of the clock face. A
pupil is selected to come up to the board with a pointer. She or he

points to each of the 12 numbers in *random* order. Each time she or he pauses long enough to elicit a correct response. After 12 answers she or he passes the pointer on to a pupil of her or his choice.

Calculator Drill

AIM: *To give pupils needed practice in adding, subtracting, multiplying (if learned, along with division).*

All you need for your "drill machine" is a hand-held calculator with a constant feature (which most have). The constant means that you can add a number such as 5 to a lot of different numbers without having to press the 5 key and the plus key each time.

Suppose you want to drill on adding 9. Press the appropriate keys for the addition of the constant 9 and hand the calculator to the child, saying, "Find out what the calculator is doing. You are to press any number key, then the equals key. Look at the answer. Keep doing this until you can tell us what you think the calculator is doing."

If the pupil pressed a 7 the display would read 16.
If he pressed a 6 the display would read 15.

After a few more of these examples he would begin to see that that the calculator was adding 9.

You can vary this for the other operations.

Pie Graphs

AIM: *To introduce pie graphs.*

Divide the class into three groups according to height. These three groupings are then represented in two forms: first, in number groupings translated into their fraction equivalents; second, in pie graph form. This will allow pupils to see the relationship between fraction equivalents and the spatial relationships that exist in the pie graph.

Ditto sheets can ask pupils to supply the fractions based on interpretation of a graph or to divide a circle in such a way as to reflect the fractions given. Don't make these too difficult.

Some third graders can be introduced to line graphs. The best line graph activities are those that measure levels of achievement or growth over a period of time. Good examples for pupils to plot are test marks, push-ups completed, or independent readings completed.

Bathroom Calculators

AIM: *To introduce pupils to the use of mechanical calculators found in the home.*

"There is a calculator in your bathroom!" This statement will really wake your pupils up. Bring a bathroom scale into your classroom. Follow these instructions and your pupils will have a beginning calculator to use.

Collect at least five one-pound and several five-pound weights. If you can't locate these easily you can make your own by filling paper bags with garden soil and sealing the bags with masking tape.

Ask the children to try simple addition and subtraction problems with the weights and show them how the answers can be read on the scale.

Zero Fraction Game

AIM: *To provide practice in multiplication in game form.*

Construct a game board by copying this simple number strip. Add a pair of dice.

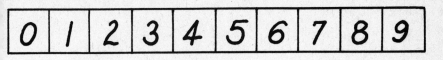

Begin at zero. Roll two dice and multiply the numbers you roll. Move to the square representing the last digit of the product. On your next turn add your last digit to the square you're on and move to your new last digit.

The first player to get back to zero wins.

Any number can play.

Hint: Convert this to a fraction game for older pupils.

Examples:

Dice Roll	Product	Square
4,4	16	6
1,6	6	2
1,4	4	6
6,6	36	2
1,5	5	7

Magic Squares

AIM: *To provide practice in adding columns.*

8	1	6
3	5	7
4	9	2

(In a "magic square" the sums of the rows, columns, and diagonals equal the same number.)

Draw a 3 by 3 square and fill it in by multiplying each number in the square on the preceding page by 2.

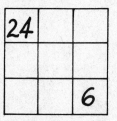

Now fill in a square by adding the two magic squares.

Is the result also a magic square?

Guess-timation

AIM: *To provide pupils with opportunities to guess or estimate a correct answer.*

Use real life situations to provide your pupils with estimating practice.

1. Suppose your math book were 12 inches thick. About how many pages would it have?

    Hint: Measure your math book and check its pages.

2. How many grains of breakfast cereal are in a cup?

   Hint: See how many are in a spoon. How many spoons in a cup.

3. What would be the total weight of all the pupils in your class?

   Hint: How many rows or clusters are there in your class? What is the weight of one row or cluster?

4. How many ounces of soda pop in a case of 12 bottles?

5. How many minutes in a full seven-day week?

Roaming Roman Numbers

AIM: *To provide your class practice in handling Roman numbers.*

Discuss Roman numbers. Display some examples such as the face of a clock, the cornerstone of a building, and the chapters of a book.

Collect story titles and familiar expressions that have numbers in them. Write them on the chalk board, substituting Roman numerals for written-out numbers or Arabic numerals. For example:

A cat has IX lives.
Behind the VIII ball.

Then hand out a sheet with fill-in questions, the answers of which are Roman numbers.

_____ Little Indians
A stitch in time saves _____
_____ and _____ blackbirds, baked in a pie.
_____ little pigs

Catalog Math

AIM: *To provide a board game that combines fun with math skills practice.*

Use a large square of bristol board or cover an old folding board from a discarded board game. This problem-solving game gives practice in making purchases, figuring change, and using a catalog. The board game format adds interest. Players begin with a given amount of money and make the purchases indicated by the dial on the game board. They must refer to the catalog to find the selling price. The pupil with the most money at the end of the game is the winner. You will need a Sears-type catalog, game board, markers, paper money, coin chips and a tax chart (optional).

Lost and Found

AIM: *To provide basic skill practice, using question marks for the missing digit.*

Prepare oaktag charts with simple and more complex numerical problems with some numbers "lost" as indicated by a question mark. Try it with a variety of operations.
Example:

$$6 = 2 + ?$$
$$? - 3 + 1 = 6$$

3 ?	Answer:	3 6
× ? 4		× 2 4
1 4 ?		14 4
? 2		72
8 ? 4		86 4

Mindreading Math

AIM: *To give pupils practice in doing mental arithmetic.*

Tell the class that you can read their minds. Explain that they are going to choose any number from 1 to 100 and if they follow your commands you will know what number they wind up with.

Commands:
1. Add 10 to it.
2. Double your answer.
3. Add 100.
4. Take half of the result.
5. Subtract the number you started with.

At this point announce that you know the resulting answer.

If they have done all the operations correctly, the answer will be 60.

Name What's Missing

AIM: *To increase the ability to solve verbal problems.*

Point out to your pupils that to solve a problem you must have enough facts. Read this problem.

John delivered 70 papers on Sunday. How many papers does he deliver in a week?

What is missing? You cannot answer this question because you do not know if John delivers 70 papers every day or just on Sunday.

Ask pupils to list what information is missing before they can solve any of these problems.

1. Maria spent 50¢ on a comic book. How much money did she have left ?
2. Henry got up at 7 A.M. How many hours did he sleep?
3. Mrs. Smith had two cups of coffee for breakfast. How many cups does she drink in a day?

Then ask the pupils to supply the missing facts and exchange problems with a classmate.

International Math

AIM: *To reinforce basic math skills using international currency exchange.*

Divide your class into buyers and sellers, with approximately equal teams. Teach the names of the basic currency in several countries. Make a chart that rounds off, very roughly, the value of these foreign currencies with the dollar. For example:

$1.00 = 5 French francs
$1.00 = 550 Italian lire
$1.00 = 60 Spanish pesetas
$1.00 = 3 German marks

You may want to reverse this chart as well: 5 francs = $1.00, etc.

The sellers then cut out pictures of basic items from a department store catalog, leaving the price in dollars. The buyers cut up strips of colored paper and make facsimiles of the foreign currency. The fun begins when the pairs of buyers and sellers begin to haggle.

Bird Feeder Arithmetic

AIM: *To combine nature study with basic arithmetic skills.*

Set up a bird feeder this winter. Use these realistic questions to develop your pupils' appreciation for math skills.

1. How much birdseed was used today?
2. How much was used over a two-week period?
3. What was the average per day during the two-week period?
4. What is the weight of a bag of seed?
5. How many days should a bag last?
6. What is the cost of a bag of seed?
7. How much is that per ounce?
8. Is the larger bag a better buy?
9. How many birds would you estimate feed at our station?

Number Blocks

AIM: *To use number blocks to build numbers from random digits.*

Hand out three cards, each containing a single digit:

Then pose the following problems:

"You can build six 3-digit numbers from these cards. What are they?"

873   837   783   738   387   378

"Will 9 divide each of the numbers evenly?"

"Build six 3-digit numbers with these digits."

"Can any of the numbers be divided by 9 evenly?"

"Find three digits that give you six 3-digit numbers, *all* of which can be divided by 9 evenly."

"Find three digits that give you six 3-digit numbers, *none* of which can be divided evenly by 9."

"Can you find six 3-digit numbers that can be divided by 3 evenly?"

"Can you find six 3-digit numbers that can be divided by 2 evenly?"

For extra credit: Can you find three digits that make six 3-digit numbers that can be divided by 5 evenly?

Chinese Puzzle (tangram)

AIM: *To give pupils an appreciation of geometric shapes.*

Motivate pupils by telling the ancient story of a Chinese lord who dropped a ceramic tile onto a stone floor. The prized tile broke into seven pieces, which the gentleman spent a year trying to get back into the shape of a square.

Cut a piece of heavy cardboard into these seven shapes: two large triangles, a medium-sized triangle, two small triangles, a square, and a rhomboid. (Use the sample shown in Figure 4-2 to get scale.)

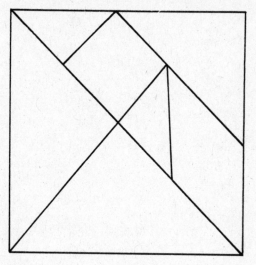

Figure 4-2

After the pupils have mastered the square, let them use their imaginations to come up with interesting shapes of their own. As pieces are manipulated, the various relationships between and among the pieces become clear.

Suggest that pupils assemble these shapes:

Rectangle   Trapezoid   Pentagon   Hexagon

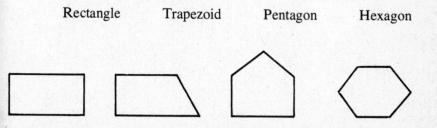

SIMPLIFIED METRIC MEASUREMENT

You have been teaching standard U.S. measurement for years. Now that our country has made a commitment to convert to metric measurement you are faced with a great challenge. Society is turning to the schools to prepare the next generation to be fluent in metrics. Again the schools, and classroom teachers, are being asked to be the agents of change.

When you take a close look at the metric system you see that it is based on the tens system. You've been teaching that whenever you taught decimals! After you master some basic prefixes and the terms for linear, mass, and volume, you are on your way.

But how can you make this new system and new language palatable to your pupils? This chapter will show you how through the use of physical activities, dice games, manipulative materials, and first-hand experiences. The games and other energizers will give you increased confidence as you accept this challenge along with all the others that experienced, dedicated teachers have risen to during the past few years.

Meter Trip

AIM: *To provide first-hand experience with meter strips.*

This is an inexpensive meter activity made from Con-Tact or other self-adhesive vinyl paper. Most brands have a measurement grid on the back. Use this to measure meter strips of equal width. Cut enough strips so each pupil has one. Remember, the pattern does not count, so buy remnants. Also, use the squares for the width; the length will be determined by metric measure. Do NOT remove the backing paper. The length is exactly one meter.

Start by having pupils become familiar with his or her own meter strip. Let them explore meter lengths in the classroom without using conversion. Have them draw three columns in their notebook and head them with these categories: Shorter Than a Meter, Longer Than a Meter, Exactly One Meter. Ask pupils to find at least three items in school or at home for each category.

Introduce the decameter by taping together 10 meter strips end to end. Explain that the metric system is based on the number 10.

You will need to go to the gym or school yard for this next activity. Have pupils place their meter strips on the floor or ground in front of them, with one end at their toes and the far end extending away from them. Now ask each pupil to discover these facts first hand: (1) How many giant steps can you take within a decameter? (2) How long does it take to hop the length of a decameter? (3) How many of your shoe lengths are there in a decameter? Let them compare answers. They will leave this experience with a good idea of what a decameter is.

If your school is near a park or open field mark your decameter strip with 11 stakes. Hammer in the first stake and call it *zero*. Stretch your decameter out from zero. At its end point, hammer in Stake # 1. Keep on going until you reach # 10. You now have a hectometer. Ask pupils to walk its length. Run races that are a hectometer in length.

Centimeter Guess

AIM:　*To introduce your pupils to simple body measure and surroundings measure.*

Prepare a ten-centimeter strip for each pupil. You can do this quickly by making one ditto or rexegraph master and running off 35 copies. Then say to your class: "Look at your centimeter strip. It shows ten centimeters. Prepare two columns in your notebook. Label one column My Guess and label the second column Actual Measure. I'm going to write the name of an object on the chalkboard. First guess how long each item is and write your answer. Later we will use the centimeter strip to measure each item. Do not think about inches. Today we are thinking in terms of centimeters."

ITEM	MY GUESS	ACTUAL MEASURE
1. Your thumb		
2. Your shoe		
3. Your math book (length)		
4. Your longest pencil		
5. The thickness of your pocket dictionary		
6. The length of your middle finger		
7. Your wrist		
8. Your nose length		
9. The width of your desk		
10. The height of your seat		

Metric Olympics

AIM: *To provide practice in using linear metric measures while in the gym.*

Adapt throwing events from the Olympics to indoor activities and measure the performances of contestants in each event in meters.

(Pupils who do not recall the Olympic events from TV can be shown a filmstrip or library book.)

For example, a balloon can be used in the shot put; a straw in the javelin throw; a paper plate in the discus throw, and a balloon on a string in the hammer throw.

After each throw the pupils measure the distance and learn the importance of accuracy as well as fluency in metric measurement.

Time each pupil running the meter-measured distances. After returning to the classroom have each pupil use his or her own personal scores for solving problems, such as, "What is your speed in meters per second?" "How far could you run in one minute if you could maintain your 100-meter speed?"

Measure the distance each pupil can long-jump and record on a graph the daily or weekly scores of each child and the class average.

Decide what form of kilometer course best suits your school setup. A regular shape—straight, circular or square—will give the best idea of the length of a kilometer. You can determine the course by using an automobile or bicycle odometer (0.62 miles). If not straight out and back, the course can go around the block or playground. Older pupils can run the total course, passing a baton to the next runner at the end of a lap. With younger pupils, station members of the group along the course, so that each runner covers only part of the distance. Chalkboard erasers can be used as batons.

Roll-a-Meter

AIM: *To reinforce relationships among metric units of length.*

This is a dice game. Make a chart showing centimeters, decimeters, and meter equivalents. Each pip or point on the die equals one centimeter. A double such as snake-eyes or any combination where each die shows the same number of dots counts double.

The first player rolls the two dice. A frozen orange juice can makes an excellent cup for this purpose. The total number of dots showing face up on the pair of dice dictates the number of centimeters he earns. Set the class up in groups of three or four players. The first player to reach two meters is the winner.

Shuffleboard

AIM: *To provide practice in adding metric units of length.*

This is an easy table-top game that you can make. All you need is a piece of plywood or masonite a half-meter wide and a little more than a meter in length. Fasten two meter sticks parallel to one another. See the diagram in Figure 5-1. Use three plastic checkers (two red and one black).

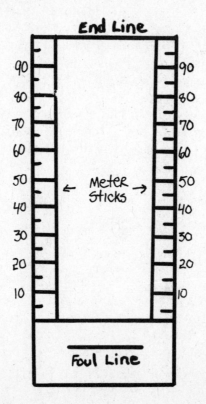

Figure 5-1

The first player slides his quoits (checkers) one at a time down the board, keeping his finger behind the foul line. A quoit that falls off the end line is voided. Quoits may ricochet off side meter sticks.

The score is computed by finding the distance each quoit has traveled. The black quoit counts double. A player must total his score and announce it in meters. The highest score after five rounds wins.

Metric Chance

AIM: *To familiarize pupils with laws of probability and multiples of metric numbers.*

This is a board game that will bring a little bit of Las Vegas into your classroom. The materials are quite simple: a board similar to the diagram in Figure 5-2 (this can be made out of oaktag, an old window shade, or an old game board that has been covered with white paint); two decks of oaktag cards, with 24 cards in each deck; and some poker chips.

Before playing make sure your pupils know that length is measured in meters; capacity or volume is measured in liters; and mass or weight is measured in grams. Review the abbreviations as well.

Use two different colors of construction paper or oaktag for the two decks of twenty-four cards. In the first deck mark the cards: .01, .1, 1, 10, 100, 1000. Repeat this so that these six numbers appear four times, totaling 24 cards in all. In the second deck mark four cards with each of these symbols: m, g, 1, .2m, 31, 20m. During play the pupil will choose one card from the top of each deck, multiply them, and return each card, face down, to the bottom of its deck. Decks should be shuffled after every few plays. For example, if 10 and .2m are picked, "2m" is the winner. If "1" and "31" are picked, "31" is the winner.

Just as in roulette, the players may place their bets on a single

30-1

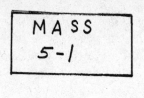

MASS
5-1

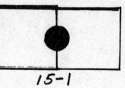

15-1

Kg	l	2 Km	3000 l
.1 g	3 l	2 mm	K l
m	Km	100 ml	20 Km
300 l	g	.2 m	100 m
cg	10 g	20 m	300 ml
dm	30 l	10 l	10 ml
30 ml	2 m	.2 Km	10 m
100 g	cm	100 l	20 mm

1 - 7

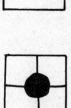

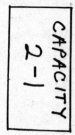

7-1

CAPACITY
2-1

Figure 5-2

3 - 1

square, on two squares, on four squares, or on a row. Another method of wagering is to place chips in the mass section (5-1), length section (1-1) and the capacity section (2-1). All odds appear on the board for the players' benefit. Betting on one number pays 30-1, two numbers (15-1), four numbers (7-1), a row of four (7-1), and a row of eight 3-1).

Start off each player with an initial bank of chips. Pupils enjoy giving the chips dollar values. Players take turns rolling the dice. After all bets are placed, the dice are rolled. Play continues for a designated period of time, with the player having the most chips declared the winner. Players who go bust drop out of the game. This game is a natural in the beginning study of probability for more able pupils. All pupils will become very familiar with the metric units and symbols used in the game.

Chain Gang

AIM: *To practice handling everyday objects that are a meter in length.*

Gather three boxes of paper clips in three sizes: #1 size, #3 size, and jumbo size. You will also need a meter stick for each pupil.

Have your pupils make a chain of #1 size paper clips, and lay them along a meter stick. They should continue to add paper clips until the length of the chain most closely approximates 1 meter. They may repeat this procedure, using #3 size paper clips and jumbo-size paper clips. They may then be asked questions like these:

1. How many clips are in the chain?
2. How many more are in the #1 clip chain than in the #3?
3. What is the length of four jumbo sized links? Is it more or less than #1 size links?

4. If no chain is exactly 1 meter in length, can you make one using a combination of clips?

Metric Crostic

AIM: *To provide skill and practice in handling U. S. and metric measures.*

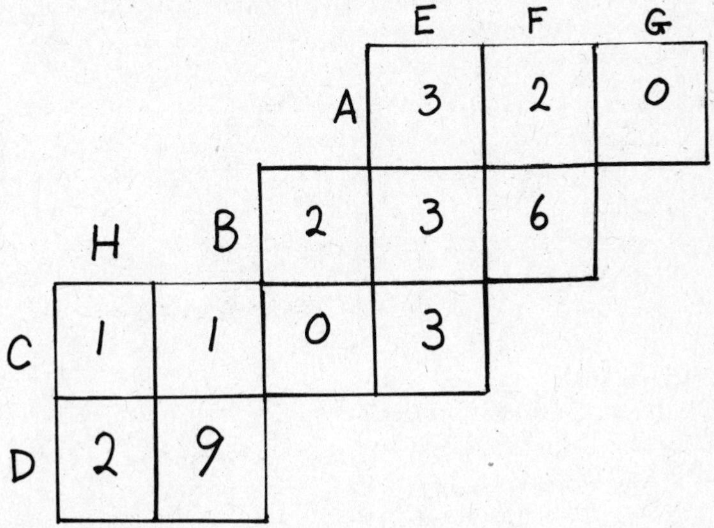

Figure 5-3

ACROSS
A. Centimeters in 3 meters 20 centimeters
B. Centigrams in 2 grams 36 centigrams
C. Grams in 1 gram 103 kilograms
D. Feet in 9 yards 2 feet

DOWN
E. Ounces in 20 pounds 13 ounces
F. Inches in 2 feet 2 inches
A. Pints in 10 quarts
H. Inches in 1 foot

Beam Pole

AIM: *To familiarize pupils with meter sticks.*

Gather boxes of paper clips of various sizes, some string, and a meter stick.

Tie one end of the string around the 50-cm mark on the meter stick and suspend the stick from some overhang. To bring the meter stick into a proper balance, you may have to insert a thumbtack at some point along the stick. Have your pupils drape paper clip chains over this balance beam. This activity gives them a chance to explore relationships between weights and distances. Using the same size paper clips, have them investigate some of the following situations:

1. Placing a 20-link chain at the 40-cm mark, how many paper clips are needed at the 70-cm mark to balance the beam? (Ans.—10 links)

2. Keeping the 20-link chain at the 40-cm mark, where must a similar chain be placed to balance the beam?   (Ans.—at the 60 cm mark)

3. If a 30-link chain is placed at the 30-cm mark, how long a chain is needed at the 80-cm mark to achieve a balance?   (Ans.—20 links)

After a few of these exercises your pupils will be familiar with the balance beam or "beam pole." Let them explore using combinations of different size paper clips for additional activities.

Encourage them to make up other problems of this kind, and to look for patterns in their solutions.

Pantry Check-Out

AIM: *To familiarize pupils with the gradual changeover to the metric system, using product labels.*

Pupils are very aware of food packages. They like the bright colors and frequently read the labels while eating the contents of the package. Many food labels already carry weight and amount in both standard units and metric units.

Ask pupils to bring to class food labels that contain both units of measure. Paste these on a piece of newsprint after you have circled the units of measure with a felt-tip marker. Have your pupils make a table in their notebook, consisting of a simple chart with three columns. The first column will be titled "Item"; the second, "U.S. Measure"; and the third, "Metric Measure." For example:

Item	U.S. Measure	Metric Measure
Canned peaches	29 oz. (1 lb. 13 oz.)	822 grams
Grapefruit sections	16 oz. (1 lb.)	454 grams
Tomato juice	24 fl. oz. (1 pt. 8 oz.)	709 ml
Chocolate bar	1½ oz.	42 g

After the pupils have added about ten items to their list, help them generalize. Ask these questions:

How is liquid measurement expressed in metric units?
How is weight expressed in metric units?
What is the most commonly used unit of measure for dry products in metric and U.S. measure?
What was the largest metric measurement you found? What was the smallest?
What does metric measure have to do with tens?

On their own, your pupils will begin to see relationships. Do not emphasize conversions from one system to another. Let your pupils discuss their discoveries with you, and with each other.

Cold Front

AIM: *To familiarize pupils with the Celsius scale.*

Gather a Celsius thermometer, jar of water, ice cubes, centimeter grid paper, and graph paper.

Help your pupils set up a chart in their notebook for recording the daily temperature readings at a fixed hour. Use centigrade or Celsius as your scale. Graph their temperatures for them on a piece of oaktag.

Now, have your pupils use 1-cm grid paper for their own graphs. This kind of paper will give them familiarity with this important metric unit. Some pupils will want to draw a double bar graph, comparing the inside and outside temperatures.

After they feel comfortable with this scale, try this. Pour a small amount of tap water into a jar and determine its temperature. Then fill the jar with a dozen ice cubes. At one-minute intervals, a temperature reading should be taken and recorded on a simple table on the chalkboard. At their seats, pupils can convert the board chart of falling temperatures with a simple line graph on graph paper at their desks.

Here are some suggested questions you can ask:

1. What happens to the temperature as the ice melts?
2. What is the lowest temperature reading we got?
3. What happens to the temperature after it reaches its lowest point?
4. Did the water ever reach 0°?

—6—

SOCIAL STUDIES . . . WITH A DIFFERENCE

The program of social studies in most schools has two main sources of content—the daily experiences of the pupils and the broad topics from which learning experiences are developed. In order to succeed in teaching social studies it's important to use approaches and activities that are concrete and close to the everyday situations with which your pupils are familiar. Important current happenings and present aspects of the topics studied should be included. Just as important is a "feel" for the subject.

This chapter will help you achieve their goal. By using the concrete, practical suggestions you will be able to "turn on" even the most reluctant learner to the world around him. For example, your pupils will acquire map skills, increase their social studies vocabulary, search their roots, role-play American history, understand the role of law, and develop many other attitudes and skills.

Simulating different times in our history and acquiring geography skills will equip your pupils to further enhance their understanding of the world around them. As experienced teachers, you and I know that social studies is taught differently in every school. In some places it is a vague catch-all of isolated information. The material you find in this chapter will help you pull it all together. At the same time it will stimulate your pupils to think.

How Long—How Far?

AIM: *To comprehend that places are different distances from where we live.*

Ask your pupils to name places where they go shopping with their parents (mall, department store) or ask where their relatives (grandparents) live. They identify the distances in any terms they can, such as two buses, three train stops, a little time in the car, all day, etc. Responses in any terms of time or distance are acceptable.

Help your pupils begin to develop a sense of distance. Use gradual comparisons. It takes longer to get to Bradlees than it does to Ward's. It is further to Springfield than it is to Newtown.

After some experience, your pupils will begin to become more precise. Encourage them to speak in terms of miles or minutes, and then list the places in terms of nearness. Ask the children to get help from their parents in listing where family or friends live. Help pupils construct a chart in their notebooks, listing places in terms of nearness.

Service Coupons

AIM: *To help pupils develop habits of citizenship.*

You can make aspects of good citizenship come alive for your pupils by designing a simple "Citizen Coupon Book" for each pupil. Of course, you will emphasize that there are satisfactions from doing good without any tangible reward.

Begin by designing a simple coupon that can be duplicated on the ditto machine. Leave room for the pupil's name, class, and type of service, as well as the signature of the person served. Start each child off with a booklet (he or she makes the original cover) of 10 or 12 coupons. Discuss with the class the kinds of service or good citizenship they can demonstrate, such as running an errand, caring for another person, helping a school visitor. As the youngsters get their coupons signed in or outside of school, have them bring the signed coupons to class. Once or twice each week, discuss the varieties of service performed.

Directions Game

AIM: *To teach pupils how to use the four directions (north, south, east, west).*

All you need for this wall game is a 22" × 28" piece of cardboard, two thumbtacks, and some small pictures.

Rule the board into two-inch squares. Place it over a cork bulletin board or other soft surface. Have pupils scan magazines and cut out small pictures (2×2) that appeal to them.

Call a child to the ruled board and ask him to place his picture (dog, car, house, etc.) in any square he wishes, securing it with a thumbtack. He then places another picture, this time of a person (baseball player, pilot, nurse) in a distant square. The child at the board now calls on a seated pupil to give directions as to how the nurse can get to her car, using terms like "go two squares north and three west." If the child called upon gets the directions correct, he or she now comes to the board. Incorrect responses means that the child has another turn.

Election Word Find

AIM: *To help pupils use the vocabulary associated with local and national elections.*

Say to the class: "Words that remind us of elections are hidden in the block below (Figure 6-1). See if you can find: President, office, White House, election, campaign, November, Republican, political,candidate, congress, governor, banner, ballot, vote, Democratic."

Be sure you spend some time defining these words and using them in sentences.

```
CAMPAIGNVOTE
AWHITEHOUSEJ
NNBGOVERNORP
DOVELECTIONR
IVICONGRESSE
DETRBANNERPS
AMOVOFFICEOI
TBNNBALLOTLD
EEPOLITICALE
QRREPUBLICAN
UDEMOCRATICT
```

Figure 6-1

The Food Game

AIM: *To demonstrate the interaction of food.*

You will need pictures of plants, animals, and environmental factors such as sun, water, soil.

Have each child pin one picture to his or her clothing.

Pause to have pupils look at one another's pictures.

While they stand in a circle (a group of eight is best) the teacher hands out six feet of colored yarn to half the pupils. Pupils with yarn look to see a relationship between their picture and one other. He or she hands the other end of the yarn to the pupil with a picture that depicts a relationship. Let this continue until all connections have been made. Now give similar lengths of yarn to the pupils who did not get it originally. These pupils now connect themselves to pupils picturing a relationship with their picture. They have now created an intertwined food web. Then ask them to close their eyes and pull the yarn between them as tight as they can. Reach into the center of the web, press down firmly, then let go suddenly. This dramatically illustrates that an impact at one point of the food web is felt throughout the entire system.

Compare this effect with the real world of food. As an outgrowth of this game, ask the pupils how all the pictures can be related to the sun. Have them look around their classroom to find items related to the sun.

Giving Directions

AIM: *To improve the ability of early grade pupils to give directions.*

Pair off your class. One member of each team thinks of a place somewhere in the school. He or she does not tell the other team member the place chosen.

The "directors" (those who have thought of the location) write down directions telling how to get from the classroom to the place they are thinking of. They use only words, no pictures or drawings. Encourage them to tell things like:

Which way the person should go (left, right, up, down).
What the person will pass (fountain, office).
How far the person should go (all the way, halfway down the hall).

The directors now hand the papers to the "seekers." The seekers may ask questions of the directors. Only questions of clarification are allowed.

Permit two or three pairs of pupils to leave the room in search of their quest.

Enrichment: Have several pupils write directions for finding the same place. Compare.
On separate pieces of paper, write directions and make maps for getting to some location. Hand the written directions to one pupil and the map to another. Who is the first to locate the spot? Discuss which is easier to use and why.

Urban Geography

AIM: *To help city children understand direction.*

Review the concepts of north, south, east, and west with your class. Then ask your pupils to suggest places of interest in their community that a visitor might inquire about. List these on the board. Include items such as housing projects, police station, library, fire house, supermarket, department store, etc. Using the school as a starting point, ask one pupil to direct a visitor to one of the places you listed on the chalkboard. Answers must contain phrases like "one block north and two blocks east." You can divide the class into teams and they can quiz one another.

Relay Race

AIM: *To help pupils categorize the knowledge they have learned.*

One of the frustrations teachers face is that pupils have difficulty putting the information they have acquired into appropriate categories. For example, an otherwise bright child, when listing the names of states, may come up with "Philadelphia." A pleasant way to practice categories is with a chalkboard relay race. It works like this:

Divide the class into relay teams with equal numbers of students—say, six teams of five students each.

The teacher writes six different categories (or as many categories as there are teams) on the board. Use famous cities, inventors, presidents, states, world capitols, explorers, rivers, mountain chains, lakes, etc.

At a signal from the teacher, the first player in each line writes in something that fits the category. Then he or she hands the chalk to the next player, who is waiting at his or her seat, and is seated.

The rest of the players do the same thing until the whole team is seated. The first team seated whose answers are ALL correct is the winner.

Roots

AIM: *To further your pupils' appreciation of their community's historical background.*

Make a list of your community's historical monuments, statues, or markers. List them on the chalkboard.

Assign a small committee of pupils to research the item by finding out the following:

What event does the market represent?
What happened?
Who was there?
Where did it happen?
When did it happen?
Did the event have any effect on the people in the community?

Check out the library to see if there are any books on an appropriate level for your pupils to look at. Ask if the Chamber of Commerce has any material. Obtain it for your committee's scrutiny. Have committee members give a chalk talk.

Curtain Call (Role-Playing)

AIM: *To combine the pupils' love of make-believe with a study of roles in American history.*

This activity will energize even the most sluggish group. It does require a little homework on the part of the teacher. Prepare a few skit outlines at home and have them run off on the ditto machine. Distribute them to the entire class and then ask for volunteers to come up and improvise from the brief skit outline. Some ideas for inclusion are:

Two pupils are seeking the nomination of their party for President of the United States. Have them make speeches and develop a platform.

A Georgia farm boy comes home to tell his mother that he wants to join the Confederate army.

An Alabama slave owner wants to free his older slaves. He discusses this plan with his neighbors.

Role-playing can be just as effectively used for current events. What about pollution? One pupil is a manufacturer of chemicals. Another portrays the role of a consumer advocate.

Your role-playing sessions can gain sparkle and lots of student humor if you add commercials in between skits. Pupils love to parody familiar commercials when they write their own. By all means encourage them to be creative.

You will find that the number of situations is endless. The only limits are your imagination and your class' energy.

Map Puzzles

AIM: *To further pupils' understanding of spatial relationships.*

Every school has some old maps that they no longer want or use. You can help your administration out with this energizer.

Mix up some white glue and water. Paste the old maps onto large sheets of plywood. Ask your custodian or some cooperative father to use a jigsaw and cut the map into puzzle pieces. If it is a map of the United States, try to retain the states' shapes. For other maps, any jigsaw shapes will do.

Now roll down the new maps and have the pupils compare the shapes while constructing the map puzzle on the floor. Older children can do the same with maps of Europe and Africa.

Did I Know That?

AIM: *To help pupils see graphically just how much they learn during a social studies unit.*

Before studying a unit, such as a country in South America, call on pupils to tell the teacher all they think they already know about the country—the people, language, foods, cities, climate.

The teacher serves as "secretary" and a pupil is called upon to give his or her response to the above items. These replies are written out by the teacher-secretary and sealed in a "time capsule." The time capsule can be an empty cereal box that is sealed with tape and buried at the bottom of the teacher's coat closet. There it remains until the end of the unit, at which time it is opened and read aloud by the pupil who responded initially. Pupils enjoy hearing their former misconceptions. When recent research points out that some of their earlier ideas are indeed correct, the pupil frequently responds with,

"Did I know that?" Either way, it helps pupils to see just how much they do learn during the study of a unit.

Border Patrol

AIM: *To introduce the concept of national borders.*

Have each pupil find a place in the classroom that is "my island." Ask them to draw a chalk border on the floor around their island.

Next, place four bags of cookies in random places throughout the room. Inform the pupils that the cookies represent resources needed for survival. To get the resources they could negotiate with other students for a pathway, or combine with other students, forming nations that surround resources.

When the process of border expansion and nation building is finished, introduce terms such as empires, nationalism, annexation, and federation.

Point out the convenience of natural borders (rivers, mountains) and compare them with the floor borders.

Simulations

AIM: *To create more in-depth research in history through a fun format.*

Try using "You Are There" simulations as incentives for fifth and sixth graders. Let the children portray characters and events by playing the actual roles of the people involved. To actually simulate Columbus, Washington, Betsy Ross, Lincoln, etc. the pupils must know the characters and their contemporaries. Then they can

put into words and actions reasonable likenesses of the actual conversations or situations. This requires them to read and study with a
definite purpose in mind. This activity will be devoured by above-
average pupils.

When one, two, or three are ready to give a monologue or
group skit based upon their studies, they will find their classmates
most anxious to listen and enjoy. The audience loves to listen critically and will lose no time in telling the performers where they were
inconsistent or made a mistake.

Crystal Ball

AIM: *To vitalize the study of "Our State."*

The usual social studies approach to "Our State" is to concentrate on geography, history and products. We seldom think of our
students as "futurists." Help them speculate about the future development of the state they live in. Speculating about the future
development can be a fascinating activity and one that draws on
much of the information pupils are already digging into as they study
their states.

Start with the year 2001 and assume that in that year the state
legislature has voted to divide the state in two. Have pupils come up
with names for the two new states. Ask them to locate a suitable city
for the capital of the second state. What kind of dividing line would
make sense? Which natural boundaries can be used? What would the
major industries be that year? What potential problems exist?

Anchor Persons

AIM: *To aid pupils in assuming the responsibility of a news team,
hence, anchor man or anchor woman.*

Form a four-person news team to present news reports once a week for two weeks. Reports should cover the local situation, national news, international news, and special reports. A recent topic might have been the rise in coffee prices.

1. Talk about where you will get information.
2. Decide what each person will do. Who will report first? How long will each report be?
3. How can the reports be made interesting? Will you use pictures, maps, or props?
4. After the first report, meet to evaluate.

Game of Chaos

AIM: *To understand the role of law in society.*

Rules and regulations are things pupils take for granted and/or view with disdain. Ask your class to imagine what changes might occur if there were no laws or rules. After a period of cheering they may begin to admit to the likelihood of some trouble and even disorder. Introduce the word "chaos" at this point and evoke some examples. List the chaotic possibilities the pupils mention according to area: school, city, state, nation.

Identifying chaos in this way may require some discussion and research. Suggest that each pupil pick a chaotic situation from each of the four areas to illustrate and caption, storyboard style, on a large piece of construction paper. These four-panel pictures become pages for a class booklet on no-rules chaos. Another page can be devoted to rules that make sense in the classroom and the community.

Conduct a discussion on differences between rules that tend to help a group and rules that tend to oppress. Pictures from newspapers or news magazines may lend authenticity to this project.

Make a Time Line

AIM: *To use a time line to illustrate a continuing problem for mankind, such as pollution.*

Man has been polluting the earth for decades. It is only during recent decades that any concern has been shown.

Develop a time line to show why people today are more concerned than ever about environmental pollution. Get a long strip of paper, such as a length of adding machine tape. Mark it off into 10- or 20-year periods. A good starting point would be 1800. Include on your time line those things that have added to our environmental problems; elicit items from your pupils:

Increase in population	[Have pupils get figures from almanac.]
Production of automobiles	[Get figures from reference book.]
Larger number of factories	[Have pupils list major pollutors.]
Introduction of jet planes	[Get precise date]
Greater use of farm fertilizers	[Get information from library]
Development of nuclear power plants	[Look up atomic energy.]

Help your pupils interpret their time line. Stretch it across the chalkboard. Do you find a bunching up of entries at a particular period of time? What does that mean?

Try to end your time line on an optimistic note. Indicate in red the dates when antipollution laws were passed. Also extend your time line into the future and indicate in red the dates when certain energy laws will take effect.

Great Lives

AIM: *To help pupils recognize milestones in the lives of national heroes.*

A class leader is selected to decide upon the name of a national figure that all the pupils are familiar with. He or she composes ten facts about the life of that person. He or she reads these facts one at a time, allowing for one guess per player after each fact is presented. Should a player guess after the first clue the name the leader had in mind, that player gets ten points toward his total score. A correct response after the second clue earns nine points, etc. If no one guesses, the leader gets ten points.

—7—

SCIENCE PUZZLES

Many experienced teachers feel insecure when it comes to teaching science. Some feel that the only way to do a good job is to conduct elaborate experiments, and they fear that their demonstrations may not come out as planned. Others feel that there is so much to know in science that they could never keep up. Still others fear that their pupils will know more than they do about some scientific phenomena. The purpose of this chapter is to give you confidence when you teach science. You need not cling to the apron strings of a textbook or packaged kit any longer.

This chapter has more than a dozen simple, fool-proof science activities, games, energizers and quizzes that you can use tomorrow. The equipment needed is always very simple and readily available. They have been classroom tested and so you know that everything will turn out the way it is supposed to.

Because the stimulating activities are geared to tease the imagination and brains of your students, you can be sure that after reading the chapter you will be asked a lot of questions—and that you will be able to answer any of the questions with confidence and poise.

Weather Watch

AIM: *To provide simple experiments and challenges.*

Pupils in all grades are aware of the weather and the effect it has on their activities. Discuss the fact that weather changes constantly, and point out that the things that make up the weather are called *elements*. Help the pupils name the elements that affect weather: wind, temperature, precipitation, etc. Ask questions like: What elements can you hear? What elements can you see? What elements can you feel?

Place several small pieces of construction paper in a pan of water and heat the water. Have the pupils observe the movement of the paper. Have them look up the meaning of *convection* to find out what this movement is called and how it explains the element *wind*.

Encourage your pupils to examine critically some weather sayings. Ask them to explain: "A fair weather friend"; "It's an ill wind that blows no good"; "Birds roost before a storm"; "Thunder will turn milk sour." Challenge them to explain the sayings and to find out if there is any truth in them.

Sprouting

AIM: *To experiment with beans.*

The sprouting of beans is a simple experiment you can perform for your pupils. You do not need soil. Your only equipment consists of a Mason jar, water, cheesecloth, and seeds or beans. (Mung beans are easy to use and easy to obtain.)

Begin by taking a quart Mason jar and covering the top with a small round screen of cheesecloth before screwing on the ring. Put ¼ cup of mung beans or other beans or seeds in the jar and fill half full with water. Let the beans or seeds soak for a few hours and then drain the water. Wrap a towel around the jar to keep it dark and place the jar on its side in a spot that's about 70°F. At home a pilot light on a gas stove gives off enough heat for proper germination. A spot near the radiator or underneath a lighted bulb is usually sufficient in the classroom.

It is important to rinse the seeds in the morning and again in the afternoon. Do this for four days. The waste products or shucks will float to the top. These should be removed. After sprouting, put the beans or seeds on clean cheesecloth and sort out those that didn't sprout.

You must rinse twice a day because if the seeds or beans are left to stand in too much water they may rot. By rinsing and adding fresh water you reduce the chance of rot. You can't crowd too many seeds in the jar as this shuts off air and induces rot. A glass container is best because you can be sure it is clean before you begin.

The best part of the experiment is the eating of the sprouts. At first some children will turn up their noses at eating sprouts. Try serving them in the classroom raw and sprinkled on buttered bread. List some of the nutritious value of sprouts. Mung beans are high in calcium, iron, phosphorous, and vitamins A and C. Barley and buckwheat are high in vitamins B and C. Soybeans are the most nutritious of all.

Have your pupils write up their experiment. Other beans or seeds you may want to try include sunflowers, lentils, unhulled oats, rye and sesame.

Glass-ful

AIM: *To provide young children with a firsthand experiment in spatial relationships.*

Get a plastic or glass tumbler and fill it with marbles. Ask your pupils whether it is possible to add more marbles to a glass already filled with marbles. After you get a *no* response, move on. If some child says *yes*, have him or her try to put more marbles in the glass.

Now ask: Is it possible to add objects (things) smaller than marbles to the full glass? If they say yes, ask which materials will fit.

Is this glass of marbles full? [Figure 7-1]

Figure 7-1

Is there space for sand? Is the glass full now? [Figure 7-2]

Figure 7-2

Is there space for water? When is the glass full? [Figure 7-3]

Figure 7-3

Group Quiz

AIM: *To help pupils understand animal groups and their names.*

Begin by pointing out to your class that people and animals live, work, and play together in groups. These groups have names, such as a *class* of pupils, a *team* of players, etc. The names for groups of animals sometimes tell what the group looks like or sounds like or acts like. Instead of saying "a lot of wolves" we say a "pack" of wolves.

After pronouncing the various group names for the pupils and making associations for them, you may want to give a "Groupie Quiz." Here are some fill-in questions with their answers:

A _____ of ants.   (colony)
A _____ of bees.   (swarm)
A _____ of geese.   (gaggle)
A _____ of rattlesnakes.   (den)
A _____ of giraffes.   (tower)
A _____ of lions.   (pride)
A _____ of hippopotami.   (bloat)
A _____ of musk ox.   (herd)

Yo-Yo Physics

AIM: *To develop basic concepts with familiar objects.*

Encourage pupils to bring yo-yos to class. Spend a few minutes having different volunteers come up front to show some yo-yo tricks they have mastered. For this experiment only the simplest yo-yo skills are needed.

Describe for the class the fabled story of Sir Isaac Newton and the falling apple. From this simple phenomenon Newton concluded that an object in motion tends to continue in motion. This is the law of inertia. Give examples of objects in motion that continue in motion even after some outside force tries to stop the motion: a child goes over the handlebars of a bicycle as it crashes into a curb; a long distance runner can't stop at the finish line; when you lock the brakes of a speeding bicycle you go into a skid.

Now have one youngster come up front and instruct him or her to let the yo-yo roll down its string and observe closely after it rounds the end of the string and climbs back toward his or her hand. Tell him or her not to jerk or move his or her hand upward as the yo-yo returns. "Why doesn't the yo-yo come all the way back up to your hand?" Ask your class to think about what natural forces might be slowing down the yo-yo. Talk about gravity.

This time repeat the sequence but instruct the pupil-performer to jerk his or her hand upward slightly as the yo-yo begins ascending the string. "Why does the returning yo-yo have no trouble climbing all the way up to your hand?" Actually the jerking of the pupil's hand applied a new force to the moving yo-yo.

Help the pupils conclude that a yo-yo unrolling down its string has acquired inertia. It would like to maintain its velocity and its downward direction. Suddenly it is acted on by an outside force— the end of the string—which forces the yo-yo to change its downward direction, but not its rate of speed. It might help to clarify the problem by thinking of the yo-yo's round trip as going down one side of the string, around the end of it, and rolling back up the opposite side. If it were not for inertia, the yo-yo would rush down the string and stop dead at the bottom. Your pupils will no doubt add that if the string is loosely knoted around the yo-yo, this will happen.

Ask pupils for other areas in which inertia bears on their lives. They have long known about it intuitively; now they can comprehend it scientifically.

Moldy Experiments

AIM: *To discover how molds grow.*

Every pupil has seen mold on bread or fruit. Talk about molds found at home. Point out that mold is made up of dozens of tiny plants in the process of growth. Molds reproduce from tiny spores released into the air from mature plants. Point out that mold spores are always in the air looking for places to take hold and grow.

Molds are parasites that take their food from something else. Unlike green plants they don't need light to grow, but they, too, must have food, water, and air. They also like places that are warm and dark. During a nature walk pupils can see that mold grows on rotting leaves, rotted wood, and tall, damp grass.

In class, pour some soda pop into two glass jars. Cover one immediately; leave the cover off the second one. In a few days mold will begin to grow in the second jar. Leave both jars in a warm place for a week or two. Mold should start growing in the first jar, too, by this time. Molds will grow quickly in coffee or tea to which sugar has been added. You may want to experiment with six jars of these three liquids, covered and uncovered. Be sure to label them carefully, including date of starting and date when mold was first noted.

You can have your children bring oranges to class. Before doing this, you should keep an old orange in a damp, airy, and dark place to promote mold. After the pupils bring in fresh oranges, pass out needles or nails. Have the pupils come up with their needles or pins to get some mold spores from your moldy orange. Back at their seats they should inject their fresh oranges with the mold spores. Have them drop the injected orange into a plastic sandwich bag with their name taped to the bag. Have them blow into the bag before sealing it shut. Place the bags in a dark place for a week or two. When the pupils re-examine their oranges they will find white spots where the injection was made. Soon the oranges will shrink and turn green with mold.

Point out that some molds are beneficial. The antibiotic, penicillin, comes from a mold. Many cheeses get their flavor from a mold that ripens them. This next experiment will demonstrate how molds make wastes disappear, and thus perform an essential service.

Discuss the problem of garbage and waste disposal. If it weren't for molds, the waste carted to garbage dumps each day would eventually bury us.

Give each pupil a glass jar that is half full of soil. On top of the soil mix in some pieces of old bread, shredded paper, orange peel, grass blades, and string. Dampen the waste material slightly; don't soak it. Some air must get in, so place the lid on top of the jar without tightening it. Every few days sprinkle the waste with warm water. Soon molds will form in different places. The waste material will become soft and eventually start rotting. Have your pupils make a journal with dates and notes on the breakdown of the waste material. Eventually all the waste will rot and become part of the soil. At this point, stir up the soil and start again. Try different materials. The presence of mold in the soil will hasten the process the second time.

Air-ful

AIM: *To exploring the invisible–working with air.*

Pupils love experiments that have an air of mystery or magic to them. This simple activity deals with air and air pressure.

Ask, "Can water be poured easily into an empty bottle?"

Set up a bottle with a one-hole stopper and funnel (see Figure 7-4). Ask the children to try to pour water into the empty bottle. Why

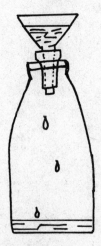

Figure 7-4

is it hard to do this? Is the bottle really empty? Many are surprised to find that very little water can be poured in. At first, a small quantity of water will enter the bottle, but then the funnel fills to the top. Why? Because the bottle is already full of air. Some water enters because its weight compresses the air, but then the air inside keeps the additional water out. This is proof that air is a real substance and takes up space.

Energy Watch

AIM: *To foster pupil awareness of energy conservation.*

Discuss with your class the three most popular sources of fuel: coal, oil, and natural gas. Point out some of the problems: air pollution, scarcity, import quotas.

Have each child explore the heating sources used in his or her house. Encourage them to ask their parents questions like: How does the heat get into the rooms of our house? Have we considered solar energy?

Help your pupils help their parents by preparing this energy watcher quiz:

1. How many windows are there in our house?
2. How many have storm windows or thermopane?
3. How many have putty in the cracks?
4. How many have heavy drapes that open and close?
5. How many doors do we have in our house?
6. How many doors let air in under them?
7. How many have weather stripping?
8. How many rooms do we have in our home?
9. How many rooms have floors with no covering?
10. Do we close the doors of rooms not in use?
11. Do we close windows when leaving rooms?
12. Do we lower the thermostat at night?

Your pupils will enjoy filling out this questionnaire together with their parents. When they return it to schjool they can pool their responses with other pupils and come up with some generalizations as well as suggestions for saving energy.

Going into Orbit

AIM: *To discover what causes an object to orbit another object.*

Gather the following materials: a large wooden spool, five metal washers, two toothpicks, a piece of string 100cm long. Push a piece of string through the hole in a spool. String four washers on one end and one washer on the other end. Tie a toothpick to each end of the string.

Hold the spool in your hand and whirl the single washer in a circle. The four washers should hang down from the bottom of the spool. Watch what happens as you whirl the single washer at different speeds.

Follow up with this quiz:

1. Suppose you cut the string while the single washer is traveling in a circle. What do you think will happen?
2. What keeps the washer in motion for a few seconds after the string has been cut?
3. The single washer traveled in an orbit around the spool. What kept the washer from traveling away from the spool?
4. The single washer acted like a planet orbiting the sun. What force keeps a planet from moving away from the sun?
5. What keeps a planet moving?
6. Suppose there were no sun. What type of path would a moving planet follow?
7. What causes a planet to orbit the sun?

Dry Ice Antics

AIM: *To see firsthand some of the properties of frozen CO_2.*

You can amuse your class and teach them some chemical properties with a chunk of dry ice. You must be careful to use tongs or wear gloves when handling dry ice. Here are some simple experiments, followed with an explanation in terms your pupils can understand.

1. Pupils see special effects on TV and in the movies which consist of eerie smoke surrounding the feet of the villain. Place a small piece of dry ice in water and watch it bubble up and "smoke."

Explanation: The very cold dry ice was not boiling in the water. Rather, the carbon dioxide gas was escaping.

2. Pupils wondered why I wore gloves when handling the dry ice. Why did it feel hot to the casual touch?

Explanation: You are not burned but frostbitten when you touch dry ice. Our nerve endings confuse the $-78°$ C temperature with heat.

3. When a metal object was put up against the block of dry ice a screech was heard.

Explanation: The screeching vibration was caused by trapped carbon dioxide molecules. The thinner the metal, the higher the pitch of the vibration. A coin placed on the dry ice will dance around and vibrate as if it were boiling.

Pollution Test

AIM: *To foster a greater understanding of air pollution.*

Gather the following materials: microscope slides (or plates of glass), petroleum jelly, masking tape, and either a magnifying glass or a microscope.

Coat one side of a slide with the jelly and hang it or place it (jelly side up) in an exposed area. Particles from the air will collect on the jelly.

Try different places to compare levels of pollution. Place slides in the school cafeteria, classroom, locker room, and general office. For homework have the pupils place slides in different areas of their homes.

Use scientific methods; that is, each slide should be exposed for the same length of time. Keep a control slide in an enclosed area like a bell jar or sealed box. Coat slides right on the site of the experiment so that you avoid picking up pollution on the way to the site.

The purpose of the masking tape is to prevent cuts from the edge of the glass. Make a frame around each slide. Use the magnifying glass or microscope to view the quantity and type of pollutants that adhere.

You will be amazed at the rational conclusions some of your pupils will come up with.

Electromagnets

AIM: *To understand the fundamental behavior of magnets.*

All children have had some exposure to simple bar magnets and U-shaped magnets. These are permanent magnets. You can really energize your science lesson by introducing a temporary magnet that has a lot of flexibility—the electromagnet. As the name implies you will need a source of electricity. No fear—a simple dry cell or two will be sufficient.

It's best to set up some small groups for this demonstration.

Fasten the bare ends of a piece of coated wire to the posts of a dry cell battery. Electricity moving through the wire causes it to become a temporary magnet. Show this by dipping the wire in iron filings. Point out how they cling.

Demonstrate that it is a temporary magnet by disconnecting one pole and watching the filings drop off. Now ask the pupils what happens if the wire is shaped in a coil of one or more loops rather than being left "straight." Help them to understand that with a straight wire the magnetic field is weak because the lines of force are spread along the entire length of the wire. When the wire is coiled into several loops there are more wires in a given area and the lines of force are closer together, with the result that the magnetic field is stronger. Even though numerous loops are wound tightly, the coil of wire is not a strong magnet because many of the lines of force move from the coil into the air. Students may discover this, but if they don't, point out that placing an iron nail inside the wire coil makes the magnetic field stronger because it concentrates the lines of force.

The coil of wire and its iron core, when connected to the dry cell, will pick up objects such as paper clips. Have the pupils try many different things to see what can be picked up. Decide together whether the iron nail has to be within the coil of wire to attract paper clips. See how long the iron nail retains its magnetism after it's removed from the coil.

Ask pupils to suggest ways to make the electromagnet more powerful. Demonstrate three ways:

1. Increase the number of windings around the same core and keep the voltage constant.
2. Increase the voltage either by using a stronger or newer battery, or by hooking two batteries in combination with the same core and the same number of windings.
3. Use a stronger core such as a larger nail or a V-shaped core while retaining the same windings and the same voltage.

Have the pupils make piles of paper clips with 10, 20, 30, and 40 paper clips in each pile. See how each of the three ways of making the magnet stronger affects its ability to pick up piles of clips.

Crystal Gardens

AIM: *To understand crystallization.*

Pupils love magic. By making their own crystals from every-day objects they see the magic of nature.

Get together a few charcoal briquettes, ¼ cup of laundry bluing, ¼ cup of table salt, ¼ cup of water, one tablespoon of ammonia, a glass bowl and a plate.

Place the briquettes in the glass bowl. Mix the bluing, salt, water and ammonia together and pour over the briquettes until they are about half covered. Put the bowl on the plate and place it where it can be observed but not moved for several days. During this period, the crystals will develop.

Try to restrain your pupils from peeking for the first day or so. You can make the crystals more colorful by adding a few drops of vegetable coloring to the briquettes.

See-Saw Physics

AIM: *To make a law of physics come alive.*

All you need for this game of live physics is a yardstick, a teeter-totter or see-saw, and a bathroom scale. Divide your class into groups of four pupils each. Weigh each pupil and record his weight in pounds. Take your class out to the playground and make a circle around the see-saw. Have two pupils from the first group sit facing each other at the fulcrum or point where the center of the beam is. Now have them move backward until they reach a position in which they are perfectly balanced. The other two pupils use the yardstick to measure and record in feet the distance of each pupil from the fulcrum. The amount of the weight and the distance are then used to calculate the foot-pounds on each side of the fulcrum. Develop the formula: distance × weight = distance × weight.

Now pairs of pupils exchange places and the process is repeated so that everyone fully understands how to equate the formula. For example: if a 90-pound pupil is four feet from the fulcrum on one side, a 60-pound pupil would have to move six feet from the fulcrum to balance the see-saw.

Becoming familiar with this formula of balanced forces exposes the pupil to the real meaning of the = sign.

Evaporation Race

AIM: *To find out about the nature of various liquids.*

Run an evaporation contest to see which liquids will change to a gas more quickly than others. Line up some identical shallow dishes—petri dishes or ashtrays are fine for this. Now divide the pupils into as many groups as you have liquids. Give each group the same measured amount of one of the following liquids: water, alcohol, vinegar, turpentine, cleaning fluid, ammonia, milk. Each group keeps a record of how long it takes their liquid to evaporate.

When all the liquids have dried up compare results. Which have residues? Which were the last to evaporate? Help your pupils to generalize about the similarities and differences among the liquids.

Does the shape of the container affect the rate of evaporation? Pour moderate amounts of water into a pie tin, a drinking glass, and a tall, narrow ketchup bottle. Make sure the amount you pour is equal. Let these three containers stand overnight and examine their contents the next day. All of the water in the pie tin and part of the water in the glass should have disappeared, while most of the water in the bottle should still be there.

Help your pupils conclude that the amount of surface area of water exposed to the air will affect the speed of evaporation.

Classroom Compost

AIM: *To discover nature's way of making humus.*

Pupils wonder about all the pretty leaves that fall from trees; what happens to them? This activity helps pupils understand how soil is made from dried vegetation such as leaves. Explain that since some things in nature change their composition, we say they *decompose*.

Begin with a wooden box six inches high in a slightly larger box lined with plastic for drainage. Put a two-inch layer of soil in the box. Over this spread an inch of crushed, dry leaves and vegetable parings from potatoes, carrots, wilted lettuce leaves, and some finely crushed egg shells. Some dead grass can be sprinkled on, also. Cover this with a half-inch of porous soil and some sawdust. Keep it sprinkled and undisturbed for a week or two.

At the end of that time, stir it up. Your pupils will be delighted to find rich, black soil (humus) that smells like a plowed field right after a rain. Repeat the process two or three times. You will now have a box full of rich soil. Plant some tomato seeds and watch them grow!

TEACHING POETRY TO YOUNGSTERS

Are you a poet who doesn't know it? Perhaps you are or perhaps you can free the poetic urges that lie dormant inside your pupils. This chapter will help loosen the restraints that may have been binding your pupils. For example. here are examples of poems that do not rhyme. You will see that rhyming words are the least important aspects of poetry. Yet, for young children some simple rhyming games are included. Limericks, haikus, cinquains, and diamantes abound, with new twists and applications for your class.

You will be able to stretch the imaginations and tease the brains of your pupils with imagery exercises. Reluctant readers will discover the poetry found in the top ten recording hits of the day. Acrostic verses will intrigue the puzzle crowd, as will the code poems.

Jump into poetry; the water is fine!

Limericks Unlimited

AIM: *To introduce a popular nonsense verse of a special form.*

Children love loony rhymes. The limerick has a special form and meter that is supposed to have come from the city of Limerick in Ireland.

Give your class just two examples of limericks and they will be on their way to making up their own. But first point out some of the basics:

1. A limerick has five lines.
2. The first two and the last lines rhyme.
3. The third and fourth lines rhyme.
4. The third and fourth lines are shorter than the other three.
5. The first line *usually* describes the place the person of the limerick comes from.

Here goes:

> There was a young man from Trevizes
> Whose ears were of different sizes,
>   The left one was small,
>   And of no use at all;
> With the right one he won several prizes.

> A man from Hoboken said, "Why
> Can't I sit on my lap if I try?"
>   He turned round and round
>   Till he fell to the ground
> And finally gave up with a sigh.

Start your class off with one or two opening lines like:

> A girl in Room Two-Seventeen
> Had a . . .

> A boy from New Jersey once said,
> "My hands . . .

Poetry Code

AIM: *To combine decoding skills and rhyming skills.*

Every pupil likes to try his skill at breaking a code. You can capitalize on this while helping your pupils put rhymes together. This one is sometimes called "Double Agent" because the code for various words is expressed as a double letter; for example, the word "bees" is written "BB," and the word "excuse" is written "exQQ."

Start them off with this couplet:

> There is a farmer who is YY
> Enough to take his EE.

When you are sure your pupils get the idea, continue:

> He studies nature with his II
> And thinks of what he CC
> He hears the flapping of the JJ
> As they each other TT.

> A yoke of oxen does he UU
> With many sighs and GG.
> Their mistakes will he exQQ
> When plowing rows of PP.

Now let your pupils try adding a stanza of their own. You can help them get started by suggesting a few coded words such as:

seLL for sells	OO for owes
smeLL for smells	hOO for hoes

The Poetry of the Top Ten

AIM: *To analyze the lyrics of the ten most popular songs of the day.*

Pupils who have trouble memorizing the words to the national anthem have little trouble learning the words of the ten most popular songs of the day. Popular music can be a unique addition to your poetry program. The pupils' interest is inherent. And the lyrics can serve as a form of literature as well as a stimulus for creative writing.

Ask your pupils to bring in to class some favorite cassettes or LPs or singles. (You may want to do some preselecting if you feel that some of the lyrics portray the drug culture or free love in a manner that might offend.) Ask the class to listen to the lyrics for content and also for style. Compare the themes to some poems or stories you have read as a class. By asking questions such as these you may be able to guide the pupils in their listening:

> What is the story or string of events the lyrics tell?
> Are the lyrics describing a feeling or mood rather than
> telling a story?
> Is there a message in the song; if so, what is it?
> How does the music help get across the lyrics' meaning?

This kind of use of popular music can be a springboard for numerous writing projects, such as:

> Translating the events of a story into a poem or song.
> Creating additional verses for the song.
> Writing parodies of a top ten song.
> Translating the events of a song into a prose story.

Feel free to experiment with the different styles of music that your pupils bring in. Nashville music will lend itself to interpretations that are different from those of movie themes or Broadway musicals.

Simile Poems

AIM: *To give pupils experience in the use of similes.*

You can get your pupils to get smiles from similes in just one easy lesson. Introduce the concept of a simile as something that is constant and natural. "Red as fire" is a simile because in nature a fire appears red in color. It would not make sense to say "red as Mary's hair," because not every Mary has red hair. Also point out that in a simile the word "as" or "like" is used to make the comparison.

Get your pupils out of the habit of insisting that their poems rhyme. Emphasize the need for imagination rather than forced rhyme. Start them off with this as a pattern:

As hot as a furnace
As hot as July afternoons
As hot as my mother's oven
As hot as a walk on the equator
As hot as the desert sand
As hot as the sidewalk in August

Next, show your pupils how to follow up on the above with punch lines. They may begin the next line with "Is the . . ." or "Am I . . ." or "Was my. . . ."

Later on, propositional phrases can be added..

Is the . . . under. . . .
Is my . . . at . . .

Or dependent clauses may be inserted:

Am I when . . .
Are the . . . where. . . .

The possibilities are endless.

Acrostic Verses

AIM: *To write simple poems, paying attention to the first letter of the first word of each line.*

Give pupils a few examples of an acrostic. They probably have done simple puzzles by now. A good acrostic to begin with is the child's name.

C _ _ _
A _ _ _ _
R _ _ _ _ _
O _ _ _ _ _
L _ _ _ _ _

Explain that the name will dictate the first letter of the first word of each line.

*C*arol is my name
*A*nd basketball is my game.
*R*unning and jumping across the gym
*O*ver and under the basket's rim
*L*eft and right goes my basketball.

The acrostic poems can be even simpler with no attention to rhyme; for example:

Johnny is my name
Only my mom says John.
Her father's name says she.
No mind say I
Neither or either
Yet I prefer John-John.

The first letters in each line may spell out a topic or activity after you have had some practice with first names. Emphasize that rhyming is not essential.

Cinquain Cinch
(Pronounced sin-cane)

AIM: *To introduce a five-line form of poetry called the cinquain.*

Review with the class the cinquefoil flower which is a member of the rose family. Point out that it has five lobed leaves. The root "cinq" means five.

Explain that the cinquain form of poetry contains five lines and generally has a 1-2-3-4-1 word count for each line. Line one contains one word representing the *title*; line two contains two words *describing* the title; line 3 contains three words *expressing action* about the title; line 4 contains words *expressing feeling* about the title; and line 5 contains one word *expressing a synonym* for the title.

Example:

Snow
Soft, pure
Drifting slowly downward
Gentle helpless icy flakes
Crystals.

Mark lines on the chalkboard to represent the word pattern. Develop with the class a class cinquain before they attempt one of their own.

Once this type of cinquain has been understood, explain that there is another form based on *syllables*. This form also has five lines and generally has a 2-4-6-8-2 *syllable count*.

Example:

Tortoise
Cute, hard shell thing
Moves so slowly, swims fast
Green little funny-designed shell
Turtle.

Haiku for Me and You
(Pronounced high-koo)

AIM: *To study the form of simple nature poems.*

Children love short, simple poems. This kind of Japanese poetry is composed of three lines. There are five syllables for line 1, seven syllables for line 2, and five syllables for line 3. The theme is usually nature and seasonal happenings. It expresses a single idea or thought. A good way to begin is to display a colorful picture. Calendar art is great for this.

Then write a poem together. Draw lines representing syllables or beats on the board. Have pupils fill them in.

Example:

Daffodil of mine
A yellow and green duchess,
Proud in the sunlight.

Emphasize that there must be 17 syllables in all. Even though the lines *needn't rhyme* the number of syllables per line must be exact in true haiku.

You can help your pupils get into the swing of haiku by drawing up lists of words that apply to a particular picture that you are displaying. This will help them find words to express their feelings to decorate their haikus with simple water colors or bold strokes of India ink to give their work a Japanese look.

Diamante Gems

AIM: *To use parts of speech with diamond shaped poems.*

A diamante is a seven-lined poem that *need not have rhyme or rhythm*, but adheres to the following parts-of-speech pattern.

The first line has a one word title or *noun.*
The second line has two *adjectives* describing the noun.
The third line has three words *describing line 1* and ending in -ing.

The fourth line has four related *nouns* about line 1 or line 7.
The fifth line has three words ending in *-ing* about line 7.
The sixth line has two *adjectives* describing the noun in line 7.
The seventh and last line is a *noun* related in some way to line 1.

This poetry form is very effective when written on a diamond-shaped piece of paper or on a kite. Here's an example:

> Humpty,
> Plump, oval
> Sitting, falling, breaking,
> Walls, kingsmen, horses, cracks
> Dropping, tumbling, cracking
> Jolly, fragile
> Dumpty.

Here is another:

> Indians
> Strong, brave
> Riding, working, hunting
> Teepees, pipes, feathers, paint
> Smoking, beating, sitting
> Colorful, proud
> Americans.

Name Rhyme

AIM: *To give pupils practice in rhyming.*

Here is a game to sharpen your pupils' ability to rhyme on the spot. Any number can play. The teacher chooses the first player, who calls out the name of a girl or boy. Within ten seconds the next player must use the name in a rhyme. If he or she can't, he or she may challenge the first player to say what rhyme he or she had in mind.

Follow this game and you will get the idea.

First player:	Paul
Second player:	Is tall, Kate.
Third player:	Has a date, Jim.
Fourth player:	Jim is slim. Mark.
Fifth player:	Is in the park. Jane.
Sixth player:	Has a Great Dane. Ann.
Seventh player:	Uses a silk fan. Mary.

This game teaches your pupils how to make rhymes and it is good for laughs as well. Notice that some pupils used the name as part of the rhyming sentence and some did not. Either way is good.

Couplets

AIM: *To help pupils versify.*

This game is best played with two players at a time. The pair sit facing each other. At the same time, they first clap their hands once, then slap their thighs. Then they snap the fingers of their left hand. Finally, they snap the fingers of their right hand.

After they practice this for a few minutes you add a new dimension. Tell them that you will recite a line and the first pupil must repeat it while going through the slapping, snapping motions. As soon as he has finished, the second player must go into the slapping, snapping motions and make up a line that rhymes and makes some kind of sense. After the second player has matched a line or completed the couplet he or she recites a line of his or her own choosing that the first player will have to rhyme with. For example:

Player one:	I ate some bread.
Player two:	It tastes like lead.
	I go to school.

Player One: I'm not a fool
                You can't beat me.
Player Two: Just wait and see.
                Have you a dime?

Now Player One will have to come up with a line that rhymes with "dime."

This is very much like a tennis match in that the rest of class gives their attention to one player and then to the other.

Word Music

AIM: *To foster an appreciation of the sound of certain words.*

An appreciation of poetry begins with an appreciation of words. They have beauty of thought and sound. Point out to the class that words have histories, associations, and connotations. In order to enjoy poetry, the reader and listener must first appreciate these qualities of words.

Ask pupils to think of words that have a special meaning or sound for them. You may get responses like *lullaby, velvet, molasses, tender,* etc.

Let children list five, ten, or some other specified number of the most beautiful words they know. Let them discuss their choices. Lead them to understand that the reasons for choosing are many and may vary from person to person.

Find word pictures in poems. Let children collect some of these and copy them into notebooks. Remind them of the necessity of following an exact form.

Select lines from poems and substitute "ordinary" words for the more picturesque. Compare the two.

Look for alliteration and onomatopoeia.

Let pupils keep a cumulative list of words found in their

readings, or learned elsewhere, that illustrate alliteration and onomatopoeia. Help them to note that synonyms fail to convey the
same impression because they lack the sound quality of such words.

Riddle Rhymes

AIM: *To capitalize on children's love of riddles by asking them to
solve riddle rhymes.*

Rhymes can tell a story or describe a familiar thing in unfamiliar language. "The following short rhymes describe an everyday
object. See if you can figure out what item is being described." For
a slow class or for young children place these "answers" on the
chalkboard as a clue and ask the pupils to match them with the
appropriate riddle rhyme.

> cherry   egg   teeth   bed
> candle   chimney   girl

Thirty white horses upon a red hill,
Now they tramp, now they champ, now they stand still.

(teeth)

In marble halls as white as milk,
Lined with a skin as soft as silk,
Within a fountain crystal clear,
A golden apple doth appear.
No doors there are to this stronghold,
Yet thieves break in and steal the gold.

(egg)

As I went through the garden gap,
Who should I meet but Dick Red-cap!
A stick in his hand, a stone in his throat,
If you'll tell me this riddle I'll give you a boat.

(cherry)

Invented long ago, yet made today,
Used while others sleep;
What you wouldn't give away,
And is best when neither shallow nor deep.

(bed)

Black within and red without;
Four corners round about.

(chimney)

Elizabeth, Elspeth, Betsy, and Bess
They all went together to seek a bird's nest.
They found a bird's next with five eggs in;
They each took one, and left four in.

(one girl)

Little Nancy Etticoat
In a white petticoat,
And a red nose.
The longer she stands
The shorter she grows.

(a candle)

For a culminating activity end the lesson with this rhyme that
contains four riddles:

Two legs sat on three legs,
With one leg in his lap;
In comes four legs,
And runs away with one leg,
Up jumps two legs,
Catches up three legs,
Throws it after four legs
And makes him bring back one leg.

(Two legs—a man)
(Three legs—a stool)
(One leg—leg of meat)
(Four legs—a dog)

Mr. Nobody
(Anonymous)

I know a funny little man,
  As quiet as a mouse,
Who does the mischief that is done
  In everybody's house!
There's no one ever sees his face,
  And yet we all agree
That every plate we break was cracked
  By Mr. Nobody.

Word Pictures

AIM: *To introduce pupils to poetic imagery.*

This mind stretcher teaches the imagery of color, sound, touch, smell, and action.

Read Christina Rossetti's poem, "Color." This will be your starting point for your pupils' observations of color. The pupil begins like Miss Rossetti by asking, "What is white?"

Go on to ask: What is blue . . . yellow . . . green . . . red . . . black?

Sound Imagery:

Ask: In which season (spring, summer, autumn, winter) will you hear these sounds:

the buzzing of bees
the crunch of snow
the rumble of thunder
the rustling of leaves
the fluttering of birds
the dashing of waves

Touch Imagery:

Read "The Blind Men and the Elephant" and have the pupils pick out the word imagery of touch.

Now, let pupils make up similes based on "touch" comparisons, as in the following:

as warm as _____   as wet as _____
as hard as _____   as smooth as _____
as cold as _____   as rough as _____
as soft as _____   as sharp as _____
as sticky as _____   as hot as _____

Smell Imagery

Ask pupils to match the season with these smells:

cut grass   burning leaves
Christmas pines   ripening apples
salt air   moist earth
honeysuckle vines   turkey roasting

Action Imagery

Give pupils a list of three words a poet could use to paint an action picture of the following. Ask them to supply others.

Brook   (running, babbling, splashing)
Rabbit   (scamper, leaping, hopping)
Very old man   (shuffling, trembling, tottering)

Suggest that they supply action words for these nouns:

morning
  village square
    beauty queen
      cowboy
        doctor
          schoolhouse
            churchyard

—9—

SIMPLE WAYS TO TEACH CONSUMER EDUCATION

Young people today are very conscious of money and they do not like to waste it. They are always within earshot of some radio or television commercial announcement and so are aware of the pressures put on everyone by the marketplace. This chapter will help you capitalize on these interests. All of these games, experiments, and experiences are relevant to the lives of your pupils. There are no mythical situations here.

In this chapter you will find ways to help your pupils do comparison shopping, test products, write checks, analyze advertisements, and count their change. These are just a few of the problems of daily living that your pupils will meet in a tension-free atmosphere of inquiry that we help you set up in your classroom.

Checkwriting

AIM: *To give pupils hands-on experience in checkwriting.*

Grade Five is not too soon to learn about checking accounts and how they can be helpful to the average consumer. Before you begin, visit a local commercial bank. Tell them that you want to introduce your class to the benefits of a special checking account. They will give you a quantity of deposit slips and enough blank checks to take care of your class' needs.

Motivate your class by writing a separate check payable to each of your pupils for $1,000. This will cause their eyes to sparkle when you dole them out. To add a little interest, sign a fictitious name to each check, like John van der Mint or Dolly Dollarsign.

On the chalkboard draw a facsimile of a check and explain the important parts, such as date, payee, amount (in numerals and words), signature. Explain what an endorsement is and how money is added to an account. The bank may give you some monthly statements from closed accounts so that your pupils will see how a tally is made of checks written.

Inevitably the question of overdraft is raised by a pupil. If it doesn't come up, ask the pupils how they think such a situation is handled. You may get some amusing stories of how overdrafts affected their own households.

Reward pupils for work that they have done in the classroom, or achievements they made academically, by depositing sums in their accounts ($1.00 for every point earned on a math test or $25.00 per month for watering the plants). Explain that fines will be levied against pupils who violate class rules; these fines must be paid by check. Every month assign pupils the job of preparing a statement for homework.

This is one assignment your pupils will enjoy and recall for years to come.

Consumer Law

AIM: *To acquaint pupils with laws that protect them from fraud.*

Ask pupils to look up the word "fraud" in the dictionary. Someone is sure to paraphrase the formal definition with the term "rip off." Add examples of fraud as it affects consumers. With a little encouragement the pupils will tell stories of their parents' encounters with fraudulent merchants. Assure your pupils that consumers can do something about this. Help pupils to use their telephone book to get the names of Consumer Action and Consumer Protection agencies. Compare their functions with those of the Better Business Bureau.

Bring in advertisements from newspapers and magazines. Together with the class, analyze advertisements for tricky words and words in small print. Have pupils make up their own ads, using large sheets of white paper. Encourage them to use colorful words and letters to capture the reader's eye and imagination.

Ask pupils to bring in a warranty or guarantee that they received with toys or clothing they bought. Explain that a warranty is a guarantee that assures the property will be presented as promised. Why is it important to read a warranty before you buy the item? In case of fraud, whom should you contact?

Hold a swap shop in which pupils bring in, and trade with one another, items from home. Make it a requirement that a warranty or guarantee accompany each item. These should be written by the pupils in class. Elect a Small Claims Court with three judges. It will be their function to hear all complaints regarding faulty toys and games that have been traded.

Suggest that pupils write a law that would protect them from unscrupulous manufacturers. When the class is satisfied with a single law, send it in to a state legislator. Your pupils will be thrilled with the reply.

Let the Buyer Beware

AIM: *To help pupils use good judgment in buying toys.*

Just before Christmas the TV commercials as well as newspaper advertisements assault young people with propaganda about particular toys and games. Sadly, many children build up a desire for a particular item without really knowing if they will enjoy using it.

Help your class to draw up a checklist of criteria that pupils can use when asking for a particular toy or game. Here is one for starters:

1. Is it well made or likely to break?
2. Will I need batteries to make it work? Are they included?
3. Are bulbs or other parts needed?
4 Are the directions for use easy to understand?
5. Will I need tools or adult help to put it together?
6. Can I take it apart once it is assembled?
7. Does it look as though it will break easily?
8. Can I obtain parts later on if needed?
10. Is the size of the box or packaging misleading?
11. Is there any danger to my younger siblings or pets?
12. Will I tire of it easily?

By reviewing each of these items and applying them to various toys and games on the market you will help your pupils make wise decisions for themselves.

Ask pupils to bring to class examples of deceptive packaging or poorly made toys that they received at some other time. This will be a good lesson for others to learn.

Parents will thank you for this activity.

Market Research

AIM: *To introduce pupils to the concept of consumer acceptability and product development.*

Suggest to the class that they are all food technologists working in a large laboratory. It will be their job to find out what people would like to buy in the way of a breakfast cereal. This information will be used to create a new product.

To help the pupils understand the process, divide them into two groups. One group will develop a questionnaire and will go into the community to determine just what it is that people would like in a breakfast cereal: taste, size, color, price. The second group will research the kinds of grains, flavors, and ingredients as well as processes that can be used to come up with a product that will meet the needs discovered by the first group.

List on the chalkboard the attributes of this make-believe food. Point out why certain ingredients would not be practical. If they develop a chocolate covered cereal, it will be hard to store, the chocolate may soften and clump, and it may be too fattening for most people.

The best part is when the pupils try to come up with an original name for the product. Some will be funny, others merely descriptive. The name will probably reflect what seems to be the biggest need as discovered in the market research.

Remind the class of the concern many people have for food that is healthful as well as tasty. Ask the more artistic pupils to design a package. Select a committee to write advertising copy.

Test the product out on another class as to acceptability. Is the name catchy? Is it original? Do the ingredients sound appetizing? Would they buy it? Is there a similar product on the market?

Who knows where an activity like this may lead? General Mills or Kelloggs may come knocking on your door.

Community Stores

AIM: *To provide first-hand experience in evaluating local shops.*

Older elementary school pupils love to do their own shopping. What's even more fun is to swap impressions of local shops, whether they are found in suburban malls or along city streets. This is a great opportunity for primary research. Help your pupils compile a consumer resource guide to neighborhood stores.

Start off a class discussion by asking where pupils could buy a frying pan in a local store or mall. Lead into a discussion of a guide book that would help newly arrived neighbors. Together come up with the kind of information that should appear in the guide book: store name, address, phone, type of merchandise or service, name of the owner or manager.

Take the class on a walk, with specific assignments for each pupil. A week in advance distribute a single-sheet flyer to the owners of the stores advising them of the project.

In class and prior to the trip go over with your pupils the elements of a good interview. Stress courtesy and the fact that these will *not* be critical reviews but solely information-seeking. Pupils may decide that they would rather distribute a questionnaire to each store owner and then collate the responses.

After the trip or collection of data begin to think of the format of the guidebook. What categories of shops will you list? Will it be geographical as well as by type of store? What form should the publication take, mimeo or ditto? What will the distribution be?

This is a very practical kind of language arts, social studies, consumer education, economics lesson. The action research is combined with a publishing venture.

Because of the free publicity offered, the businessmen should give you complete cooperation. Best of all, the action takes place right in the backyard of the class. Parent interest will be high also.

TV Commercials

AIM: *To analyze and evaluate TV commercials.*

"Do you get what you see?" can be the theme of this mind-expanding activity. Ask your pupils to compare some specific products with the claims made for them on TV. This will lead to better shoppers who will think critically rather than impulsively.

Start with commercials for games that look great on TV but turn out to be "small" in a "big" box. From this close-to-home area you can move on to automobiles. This is another area where pupils have some first-hand experience as riders and observers and feel that it is relevant.

Now you are ready to set up committees. Each committee can study a separate product. They can legitimately tell their parents that they have to watch TV for homework. They should watch for their product on television (or in newspapers and magazines). As they watch, they note the claims made for their product. Explain that they will follow up by researching the accuracy of the claims. In some cases they will perform the tasks shown in the commercials to see if the product does in fact live up to the claims.

As a culminating activity, the committee writes an accurate, truthful commercial for their product. Some committees get so involved that they actually write to the manufacturer to tell them about their findings—both good and bad.

Here are some popular committee areas that have been studied with success. Put them in question form to provoke pupil interest.

1. Does *Head and Shoulders* remove dandruff?
2. Do *Pampers* keep a baby drier than cloth diapers?
3. Does *Crazy Glue* really support the weight of a man?
4, Do *Bounty* paper towels actually absorb better than other brands?
5. Do dogs prefer *Gainesburgers* to other foods?

Making "Money"

AIM: *To provide pupils with facsimiles of real coins.*

Intermediate grade pupils like to touch and feel coins or facsimiles of coins when they are talking about money or computing money problems. Here is a simple energizer that you can do with readily available materials. No doubt you have heard about "rubbings." Gravestone markers and city manhole covers have been copied by rubbing over them with paper and crayons.

Follow these simple rules and watch the smiles on your pupils' faces:

Use masking tape to attach pennies and nickels (or other coins) to a sheet of paper. Turn the paper over and demonstrate how an image of the coin is created by gently rubbing the area over the coin with a crayon. You may want to use an orange crayon for the pennies and a gray crayon for the other coins to give them some resemblance to their true color.

Don't worry about placement on the sheet. Your pupils will cut out the "heads" and "tails" of each coin and paste them together to finish the coins. You may want to show them how to sandwich a piece of thin cardboard between the two paper surfaces. This will give your coin more body.

There are many ways in which you can use the "coins" in your class: a class store, math lessons, rewards, a class bank, etc. You can even make money worksheets for the whole class by using carbon master rubbings for duplicating machines.

Be sure to point out the difference between making "play" money like this and attempts at making counterfeit money. This is a good opportunity to discuss the physical characteristics of real coins. Why do the edges of silver coins like dimes and quarters have lines or milling on their edge? (To discourage filing.) Why is there orange along the edge of quarters? (Copper alloy sandwich inside to save silver.) What does the letter next to the year mean? (Mint coin comes from.) This is a good time to introduce coin collecting as a hobby, also.

Shopping List

AIM: *To help pupils budget their money and shop wisely.*

Most metropolitan and suburban newspapers contain pages and pages of food advertisements on certain days each week. Ask your pupils to bring in the food pages on Thursday morning.

Ask each pupil to plan a tentative menu for the following week for his or her family. Ask them to jot down the various food and cleaning items they will need. Set up small groups of three or four pupils to act as a family or purchasing group. Every group must decide to spend the same amount of money for the shopping trip. Start them off with $40.

Each group must cut out a specific ad or "special coupon" from the paper and write on it the quantity that will be purchased. Each committee then tallies up the amount that will be spent. Some pupils will realize that they can save money if they go to different stores for different items. All groups must figure out what they need, how much they need, and how much money it will take.

When each group is finished, they report to the class as a whole. A vote is taken on the committee or group that did the best job. Beforehand, certain criteria are established on what constitutes a good job. Some items we have gleaned are variety of food, money left over, quality of "real" food, etc.

A similar game can be played with clothes and hardware ads. One teacher we know brought to class a clutch of catalogs. Small groups and individual pupils went "clothes shopping" for every change of season, using the catalogs. A "fashion show" was held to model what a family could buy for $200.

Children exposed to these shopping experiences will certainly be better-informed consumers.

Madison Avenue

AIM: *To read critically ads that promote health and beauty aids.*

Every magazine and much of TV advertising is geared to improving the appearance of health of readers and viewers. Gullible people today are still being taken for millions of dollars. Sadly, people living on the edge of poverty are frequently the first to be "ripped off" by misleading advertising in this emotional area.

While most advertising is responsible and ethical there are many questionable ads in the area of health and beauty aids. Set up teams of four pupils each. Each group decides on a product to sell. A partial list follows to give you some idea of products or services that each team will advertise:

reducing aids	hair curlers	hair conditioners
muscle builders	skin creams	energy tonics
hair straighteners	hand creams	denture adhesives

Each team must tease their brains until they come up with a "gimmick." They then design a full-page advertisement to be placed in a national magazine. Before they decide on their ad they study other types of ads to determine how to have maximum emotional appeal.

Hand out to each team a piece of oaktag about 12-15 inches in size. Tell the teams to use picture cutouts, different type size, and a minimum of words to get their message across. List on the board some familiar devices that are used in ads of this type: testimonials, before and after pictures, money-back guarantees, appeals to attractiveness and romance.

When the advertisements are all finished, display them around the room. Invite another class, on the same grade, to come in. Their function will be to tour the room and look at all the ads. The visiting class will then vote on the ad that they consider the most effective. This does not mean the most truthful, but rather the ad they think will pull in the most customers. Both classes will get a great deal out of the experience.

Comparative Shopper

AIM: *To give pupils hands-on experience in comparing brands.*

Ask your pupils to chose an item of processed or packaged food that is used in their home. Explain that the class is going to buy different brands of this product and compare them.

One item that worked well was a can of peaches. Here is what this teacher did:

1. Purchased six cans of peaches. While they were all of different brands, the cans were of the same size and fruit style.
2. Poured out the contents and measured the weight of the fruit and syrup combined. This was checked with the marked content.
3. Removed the actual fruit and measured its weight without the syrup.
4. Computed with the pupils the actual proportion of syrup to the total weight.
5. Checked to see if the amount of syrup varied from brand to brand.
6. Compared prices of each brand. Checked to see if any relationship existed between higher price and more actual fruit.
7. Helped class make a chart of the six brands and their prices, syrup content, and fruit content.

After this comparison test the children ate the peaches and went on to test chocolate chip cookies. Here they also compared size of cookie and taste. The teacher cautioned that taste was a relative, subjective judgment.

Parents enjoyed getting the completed tables on the various food items. Some pupils tried to see if they could make a general statement about "house brands" as compared to "national brands." They couldn't.

Consumer Lab

AIM: *To conduct a laboratory test on the absorbency of paper towels.*

The pupils understood from the start that the purpose of this lab test was to help them draw conclusions that might affect their buying. They collected samples of name-brand paper towels, including a commercial towel used in school. In addition they needed the following materials: a stopwatch, burette, flat pan, clamp stand, beaker, gram balance scale, and metal ring.

This is the test they used:

Place one sheet of paper across the mouth of the beaker. On top of the sheet, place a lightweight metal ring. Then allow a measured amount (the same for testing each sample) of water to flow from the burette's nozzle about ⅛ inch onto the sheet. (A turkey baster can be substituted for the burette.) Using a stopwatch, measure the time required for the water to be absorbed completely by the sheet. This elapsed time is a measure of the rate of absorbency of the towel. While this is going on, discuss with the class some reasons for the importance of absorbency.

To test the amount of absorbency, weigh ten sheets of a paper towel sample on a gram-balance scale. Then place these sheets together flat out in a pan of water. After the sheets have been in the water until they are fully saturated, remove them and hold them up until all the surplus water has drained off.

Weigh the sheets after they have stopped dripping. From their wet weight, subtract their dry weight. In this way the increase in their weight is determined. When this increase is expressed as a percentage of the dry weight, it is a measure of the relative amount of absorbency of this sample.

Help the pupils draw conclusions about which towel absorbed more water and which one absorbed water faster. Discuss which towel you would use in your home. Add another dimension by comparing prices. Is the additional cost justified, based on the test?

Cost of Vandalism

AIM: *To demonstrate how vandalism affects costs to consumers.*

Ask pupils what the current cost is for an ice-cream soda at a local candy store. Follow up by asking pupils what expenses the owner has and how they affect the cost of the soda. Obvious answers will include cost of ingredients, labor, rent, lighting, advertising, insurance. Help pupils understand how vandalism adds to the cost as well: money spent on repairs to damaged property, increase in insurance costs, time and labor spent on repairs and cleaning up, loss of business as customers stay away from vandalized property.

Ask pupils to give examples of how vandalism affects:

taxes
higher rents
higher prices
loss of jobs.

Plan a campaign to stem vandalism. Make posters, form clubs, plan your actions to serve as examples to other pupils. Conduct a walk around the community to inspect the neighborhood. Look for well-kept buildings to contrast with those poorly kept.

What form does vandalism take in your school community? Ask a community relations officer from the police department to talk to your class about current problems in this area. Ask the school custodian to talk to the class about some of the problems he has seen.

Counting Your Change

AIM: *To learn the quick way to count change as well as the importance of doing so.*

    Materials: Three hand puppets—man, woman, child
                 Play money—dollar bill and some change

Ask the pupils how many of them have bought something at the store and then found that they received the wrong change. Let two or three pupils tell of their experiences.

Act out the following scenario on the puppet stage, which can be any flat surface, such as the teacher's desk.

Maria is sent to the store by her mother to buy a can of juice. When she gets her change she puts it in her pocket without counting it. Once she is home, her mother sees that she has the wrong change.

Discuss what might have happened. What was wrong with what Maria did? What can she do now? What would you do? What is likely to happen?

Choose three pupils and have them act out the same story with a different ending. How did the pupil playing the child count the change? What other ways are there for counting the change (adding, subtracting). If the juice cost 76¢, how much change should Maria have?

The teacher can summarize on the chalkboard two ways to count the change in this particular transaction:

The quick way—by adding on.
Another way—subtract the amount spent. Money on hand
                  should equal difference.

—10—

CLASSROOM FUN WITH CRAFT ACTIVITIES

All children like crafts. The trick is to find projects that are within their ability and that satisfy their sense of creativity. Pupils are easily discouraged by craft projects that are "too hard." This chapter contains more than a dozen "easy" yet satisfying craft ideas that even the most inept pupil can make with his own two left hands. What makes them different is the fact that each one has a special appeal.

Many are gift ideas, some are "big," others can be done at home, and all use inexpensive, easy-to-find materials. Most are made with found materials or items that every household contains.

Your pupils will enjoy making prints with their sneakers, converting rocks into gift items, producing their own films, using leftover string, and handling simple puppets. Best of all, these ideas are not warmed-over craft ideas that you have seen over and over again. Even the most experienced teacher is due for some surprises when he or she reads this chapter.

Flip Book

AIM: *To help pupils understand how animated cartoons are made.*

Ever since Walt Disney made them popular, pupils of all ages have been fascinated with animated cartoons. By drawing repetitive pictures your pupils can make their own cartoons move. Here's how:

Hand out to each child 24 pieces of blank paper. These will be stapled later to become a "flip book." Have the pupils draw a light pencil line one inch from the left edge of each page. This is where the book will be stapled. When the pages are quickly flipped with the thumb the booklet makes moving pictures.

Through experience your pupils will discover that it takes six moves to make the flip book work. Four pictures exactly alike make up a "move." Each time you draw an object it has to be identical in size and position on the page. This point must be stressed. If the pictures are not almost exact, the motion will jump and not appear smooth.

When you want to show movement, the picture must be positioned further away from the staple or made a little larger. Make your "motion" move from left to right or up and down. As a variation, you can make a picture that shows growth instead of movement. You can make a mountain out of a mole hill or show the building of a snow man.

It is important to make simple drawings. Patience and attention to detail are more important here than art skill. Here are some ideas that have worked well for us: a sunny smile growing across a face; a super-person flying across the sky; the sun setting or rising; leaves falling off a tree; pups growing into large dogs.

Sneaker Prints

AIM: *To introduce pupils to the graphic art of print-making.*

Here is a variation to the potato print or other form of repetitive print-making. Almost every child wears a pair of sneakers to school at one time or another. There are many different kinds and brands of sneakers and each one has a distinctive sole design. The pupils will enjoy using one of their feet as an implement in creating a piece of art. The steps are easy to follow:

1. Pupils coat the shiny side of some fingerpaint paper with a single color of finger paint or tempera paint. This becomes their ink pad.
2. On the floor, alongside the "ink pad," place the piece of art or construction paper that will be the finished project. Both pieces should rest on newspaper.
3. The pupil gingerly steps onto the "ink pad," making sure to apply pressure evenly. Carefully he or she raises his or her foot and places it on the art paper. Again, care should be taken to apply pressure evenly.
4. At this point the sneaker is removed and wiped clean with paper towelling. Later it can be sponged clean.
5. The print is allowed to dry. Later, crayon, pastel, felt markers, or paint can be used to complete the print. If the print omits some lines due to sneaker wear or lack of even pressure, the pupil can draw in the missing lines or leave them alone.
6. The results will astound you with their variety. The finished prints will be as different as the pupils' finger prints. You can encourage experimentation by suggesting:

Multiple prints using the ball of the foot only.
Have pupils remove a sneaker from their foot and hold it in their hand as a printer.
Overlapping sneaker prints.
Cooperative prints utilizing two different sneakers per print.

Bead Making

AIM: *To help pupils make their own bead necklaces.*

Thanks to the American Indian and the flower children, boys as well as girls are now interested in wearing beads around their necks. This simple crafts project can also be the culminating project for a social studies lesson.

In the noodle section of your supermarket are several kinds of macaroni-type pasta products that lend themselves to bead stringing. They are inexpensive and a single box will yield enough "beads" for dozens of necklaces. These easy steps will provide your class with necklaces they will treasure:

1. Color the noodles by mixing some food color into a bowl of water. Try to stick to natural colors in earth or clay tones. By mixing blue and green you can achieve the look of turquoise stones. (Leave a few noodles natural to give a bone or bamboo look to the necklace.) Add enough noodles to soak up all the water. The different colored beads can be divided up later.
2. Spread the noodles out to dry on newspaper near the window. Putting them on the Sunday comics may give you some special effects.
3. Dental floss is an excellent stringing material. It is thick enough for young fingers to handle, and strong. Older children may be able to use elastic thread to make chokers.
4. Achieve variety by using two or three different shapes of noodles. The pupils will love alternating the different kinds of noodle-beads. Small noodle pendants can be made and added to the necklaces.

Scrap Chimes

AIM: *To make a rhythm band instrument from found materials.*

Children love to make something from found or junk materials. It is especially satisfying when the object is made from some waste byproduct that is seen everyday.

The metal pull-tabs found on soda and beer cans can be linked together. Have the pupils link strands of seven pull-tabs. Tie five of these to a thin wooden slat or pencil-thin dowel. The dowel or slat should be just long enough to hold the five strands of pull-tabs.

When this is finished, tie a string to each end of the dowel or slat so that the instrument can be hung up or held in the hand. Watch little fingers carefully to avoid cuts.

You now have a dual-purpose instrument. It can be hung outside a window or from a tree branch to be moved by the wind to make a pleasant sound in a garden or yard. The aluminum tabs are impervious to weather. The scrap chimes can also be used as part of a spirited rhythm band. The child grabs the string handle and shakes the chime manually.

Bread Sculpture

AIM: *To develop children's interest in sculpture with an easy, inexpensive medium.*

Clay, kilns, and glazes are sometimes frustrating for young children. You can now provide them with the satisfaction of sculpture at low cost and without long waiting periods or accidents while firing. There are only three simple materials: bread, water, and white glue.

Have the pupils bring in stale pieces of white, packaged bread slices. Remove the crust and break the bread into small pieces. Add one tablespoon of glue for each slice and knead until the mix becomes smooth and elastic.

In one or two minutes the pupils can begin to use the mixture to make simple statues or mini-pottery. After the forms are made and before they harden, have the pupils glaze their creations with water and glue mixed in equal parts. The next day, the hardened sculpture can be painted.

Crayon Cross-Stitch

AIM: *To provide practice in symmetrical drawing and fostering an appreciation of handcrafts.*

Bring to class some examples of carefully made needlepoint or crewel work. Show the children a piece of marked canvas and explain how the markings are followed.

Using a rexo- or ditto-master, rule lines to make a piece of graph paper with large, even boxes on it. Have the pupils fill the squares with cross-stitches, dots, or solid colors to make a symmetrical design (Figure 10-1). Encourage them to fold the paper in half and color in only one-half the design completely before going ahead to do the other half.

Tell the children to use at least three different colors. They will be careful to see that the mirror-image or symmetrical quality of the drawing is carefully executed in the three colors.

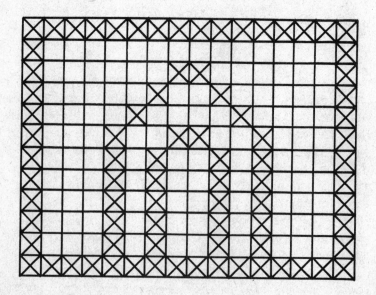

Figure 10-1

Stone Craft

AIM: *To use stones and pebbles as a medium of creative crafts.*

Virtually every elementary school child has hidden a collection of smooth stones and pebbles at one time or another. This activity will help get those stones out of the closet and into the open as pebble pictures or stone plaques.

Collect these materials before starting:

Smooth stones and pebbles of varying sizes.
Tempera paint in jars and in spray can.
White glue.
Scraps of plywood in square and rectangular shapes.
Felt in various colors, also colored yarn.
Corrugated cardboard (optional).

Give each pupil a square or rectangle of plywood or cardboard. Have them paint the background a solid color. Pass out a few matched small stones or one large stone for each pupil engaged in this project.

It might be easier to demonstrate this technique for your class using a single large stone. Place the stone somewhere on the square and glue it in place. Now trim the stone with bits of yarn and felt. If it is placed in the center of the board it may be made up to look like an Indian mask. Use felt for eyes and mouth. Yarn can represent war paint. An oval stone glued off-center can be a fish with the tail and fin made of felt and added on.

Several small stones or pebbles can be glued together to form a train or car. A small stone atop a larger one can be a snowman. Glue some pieces of cloth and yarn scraps directly onto the wood background to unify the plaque. Emphasize contrasts in color and texture of materials.

If you are using cardboard instead of wood, paste a piece of corrugated paper the same size as the cardboard to give strength and texture. This can then be spray painted.

Block Printing

AIM: *To give children experience in hand printing original designs on paper and fabric.*

Using some inexpensive materials you can give every child a chance to block print his or her own greeting cards or "signature" scarf.

This is what you will need:

White glue.
Wood blocks (from toy box).
Sheets or tapes of thin gray foam (used to insulate around doors and windows as tape; or in sheet form, used to cut and paste under heavy figurines to prevent scratching wood furniture tops).
Covered plastic soap dishes.
Bits of sponge.
Poster paint and water.
Sheets of construction paper or white handkerchief.

Begin by drawing or tracing a simple design right on the foam or its white plastic backing. Using a sharp razor knife, cut out the design. (Do this for the children.)

Paste the design onto the wood blocks. The design will be backwards which will make it right when printed.

Dampen sponge and insert it in the soap dish. This will be your ink pad. Make "ink" by mixing two parts poster paint and one part white glue.

Print by pressing the foam rubber design into the ink pad and then onto the paper or fabric. The designer's initial or symbol can be repeated all over the scarf or greeting card. Personal stationery can be made by just making one imprint in the upper left-hand corner of the paper.

String Art

AIM: *To help pupils use the elements of design along with manipulation of string.*

This is a craft activity that uses only scrap materials. All you will need are some squares of wood, boxes of nails and/or brads, and lots of string. The rest is up to the ingenuity of your pupils with a little direction from you.

Show your class a picture of the Golden Gate Bridge or some other suspension bridge. Point out the intricate network of cables.

Start off the beginners with a box of thumb tacks and some colorful yarn. Ask them to form a series of asterisks. This can be done by placing one tack in the center of a circle of tacks and connecting all of them with the yarn. Suggest that they remove the tacks and try connecting two parallel lines with a network of yarn similar to the cables holding up a bridge.

In a little while, their imaginations will run free and they will come up with their own shapes and designs. You can be of service with these suggestions for their second, more permanent, endeavor:

Wood should be thick enough not to warp and soft enough to hammer into with ease.

Nails or brads should be long enough to hold fast in the wood, yet not so long as to be distracting.

String should vary, including metallics, crochet cotton, kite cord, bakery string, weaving threads, worsted yarn, and fishing line.

On their own, your pupils will discover a knowledge of the parabolic curve and other elements of draftsmanship. Just stand out of their way and offer encouragement. By all means suggest that they try different effects, such as using nails of different lengths in the same design.

Geometric Art

AIM: *To reinforce the strength of a triangle by making a geodesic dome.*

This is a real eye-catcher! Your pupils can construct a geodesic dome using plain white construction paper. Be sure to use the heaviest bond or construction paper you can get. A visit to a local print shop will provide you with some left-over stock. You will need 20 faces for this dome, so involve 20 pupils or groups of ten pupils who will make two faces each.

Begin by cutting 20 circles of the same size, marking the center of each. As shown in Figure 10-2, fold the three arcs to the center to form a triangle.

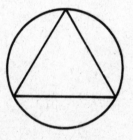

Figure 10-2

White glue is needed to connect a chain of ten circles. Now connect the first and the tenth circle to form the diameter of your dome. You have just completed the widest part of your dome. Let it dry overnight.

With the remaining ten circles, make two domes of five circles each. Join two sides of each circle to the others. You now have two completed small domes. Fasten these completed domes to the top and bottom of the original piece to complete the polyhedron. Let it rest gently on one face to dry. When dry the structure will stand by itself or can be hung. A length of nylon fishing line can be knotted and stapled to one folded arc.

These polyhedrons can be embellished by spray painting them white or silver. This will give them a little more strength and a uniform color. They make great components of a large mobile or can be used as Christmas tree ornaments.

For children who find the use of glue or paste too difficult, the edges can be stapled.

Puppet Making

AIM: *To make simple puppets.*

Check the school nurse's office or a local drug store for tongue depressors. You can also use coffee stirrers, Popsicle sticks, and paint stirrers. Have the children bring in scraps of fabric, 6" × 12" or larger.

Cross the depressors, and tape them together. Fold the fabric in half and cut a slit in the middle of the folded edge. Slip short end of puppet frame through the slit. Draw and cut out paper head with a face and suggestion of hair. Now tape the head to the front of the neck. Gather fabric loosely at the waist. Tie with fabric strip of ribbon.

You can also make "prop" puppets by looking for the animal or house picture in a magazine. Cut it out and mount it on a piece of oaktag or thin cardboard. Tape a tongue depressor or other stick to the back of your cut-out. These visuals can be manipulated from below a small-scale stage that is placed on a table top. The puppeteer sits on the floor under the table and controls the entrances and exits of the animals or other minor characters. The village or street scenes also change when these props are withdrawn or substituted. The main characters in the puppet show can be more three dimensional.

Decoupage Gifts

AIM: *To make simple presents using found materials and pictures from magazines.*

The word "decoupage" (DAY-koo-pazh) rhymes with "garage." It is from a French word meaning "cutting." All you need for this gift-making project is a pair of scissors, lots of magazines, and some odd, found materials, like small rocks, clay pots, coffee mugs, food cans, wood discs, etc.

The process takes three simple steps: cutting pictures, gluing them to objects, and coating the finished product. White glue is the best thing to use to adhere the pictures to the boxes, cans, etc. While a commercial decoupage finish is sold in crafts shops, we prefer using the same white glue mixed with water for the protective finish. Older pupils may want to use shellac or varnish for gifts that will have to withstand much wear and tear. Use a clean brush for putting on the finish coat. A 50/50 mixture of white glue and water is fine.

Start pupils off with a simple, painted rock paperweight as a gift. After finding a rock with one fairly smooth side, the pupils paint it a solid color that goes with the picture they have selected. The picture can be either smaller or larger than the smooth surface. If the picture is on very heavy paper, it should be submerged in plain water before being glued to the irregular rock surface. If the picture is on very thin paper, it should have its back painted with silver paint to prevent bleeding of its reverse-side picture. Larger rocks made excellent door stops!

Clay flowerpots can be made very decorative if they are covered with enamel first and then have pictures or bits of cloth cut and pasted on.

Coffee cans or glass mugs make good planters. Paint them first or leave plain and glue on your designs. Put gravel in the bottom for drainage.

Plastic food containers or large tin cans can become interesting food canisters when painted with enamel and decorated with a single picture depicting the food to be stored inside.

Tissue boxes when empty can become permanent, decorative tissue holders if given several coats of stiff glue to add strength. The bottom can be cut out to provide easy filling and refilling and then taped back.

Decorate shallow margarine plastic bowls. Fill with pebbles and plant narcissus bulbs or onions in them. Water. Put them in the closet for two weeks or until they sprout. Bring out into the sunlight for Christmas or Mother's Day giving.

Christmas tree ornaments can be made from plastic coffee can lids painted and decorated with seasonal pictures taken from old greeting cards. A different scene can go on each side of the plastic lid. A nail can be used to pierce a hole at the top. A bright-colored pipe cleaner makes an excellent handle.

When your pupils become more sophisticated in this cut and paste technique they can compose their own collages. A winter landscape or other realistic scene can be composed on a piece of Masonite or thin plywood.

Discarded school lunch boxes or metal waste cans can find a new life when spray painted and decorated with this technique. An attractively done lunch box can be lined with foam rubber or fabric and used as a handbag.

Fathers and mothers will enjoy getting a matching desk set that has been decorated with decoupage. Stiff cardboard makes a blotter holder, while a frozen orange juice can becomes a pencil holder. Picture frames and book ends complete the project. The use of related or matching pictures makes the various items a "set."

You will enjoy making your own items as the children work on theirs.

Film Making

AIM: *To have pupils make their own filmstrips.*

Elementary school pupils can make their own 16-mm movies, but there are many risks and disappointments for many children when this is attempted. Your own custom-made filmstrips can be fun and success is almost guaranteed. All you need is a half-frame camera such as the Olympus-Pen F. The standard 35-mm camera produces pictures too large for most filmstrip projectors. When using the half-frame camera, hold it vertically.

When you have the film processed, ask that it be developed only, not mounted. A 20-exposure film gives you 40 exposures. Five frames are needed for a leader and another five frames for a trailer. This leaves you with 30 frames for the "story." Plan each frame carefully before "shooting." You can select "directors," "camerapersons," and "screen writers" before going on location.

Some ideas are: follow-up on a field trip, how-to projects, class plays, holiday stories, highlights of the school year. Save these from year to year and delight your new class in September with a preview of what is to come.

If you think your class is up to it you can have a second group of pupils prepare a cassette tape to accompany the video. For this they will need a carefully worded script. Have them select a pupil with a clear voice to do the narration.

In order to have a smooth presentation of filmstrip and cassette, use a soft bell or chime to punctuate the end of each frame title. This will signal the projectionist to go on to the next frame.

This is a great technique to use to provide parents at an Open House with a concrete idea of what their children are doing in school. You may want to show the finished product at a mall or shopping center during American Education week.

Blueprinting

AIM: *To provide pupils with a new art media.*

Are you tired of the same old thing in art class? Why not let your pupils experiment with paper that is different? Try blueprint paper. It's something that can be used for any scene but it is especially effective for underwater scenes. Check with a local architect or blueprinter to see where it can be purchased.

The only other materials you will need are hydrogen peroxide (from the nurse), water, and a sunlamp (which is really optional).

To make a blueprint, cover desired areas of the treated paper and expose it to direct sunlight. A sunlamp will speed up the process but it is not absolutely necessary. Start out using small pieces of paper until you get a feel for the amount of sunlight needed.

When the paper is bleached to a very pale color, dip it in a dilute wash of hydrogen peroxide and water. Covered areas will become a deep blue. The longer the paper is exposed to light, the darker the blue will become.

The finished products can be framed or used as wrapping paper for special, small gifts.

Classes studying the planets will have a field day with this medium. After a unit on science fiction or a discussion of *Star Wars,* bring out the blueprint paper and see your pupils' imaginations take off!

Be sure to read the cautions on the bottle of peroxide; do not let pupils shake the bottle, drink its contents, or apply it to their hair. Also observe the suggestions for safeguarding the blueprint paper that are printed on its covering.

Detergent Bottle Viewer

AIM: *To help the pupils make a viewer for their color slides.*

Children love to make their own color slides. These can be sophisticated felt-tip drawings on glass or clear acetate, or they can be simple cartoons on oaktag or unlined file cards. Either way, they take on a special magic when seen through an individual viewer that the pupils have made themselves. What adds another dimension is the fact that these viewers are made from something their parents ordinarily throw away when empty—dishwashing detergent or liquid soap bottles. Make sure they are translucent and not opaque, since no bulbs or batteries are used with these viewers.

Cut a slot on one side near the bottom of the bottle. A razor-knife used by the teacher is good for this. Make the slit long enough for the card to be slid in and out.

Cut cardboard pieces to fit in the slot.

View the completed slides by placing them one at a time in the slot and pointing the viewer toward the light.

The kinds of slides to be made are endless in their variety. You may want to show some action in sequence, such as a trip made during the summer. Hand-drawn slides are best. Small pictures cut out of magazines can be used if pasted to the cardboard.

Hand out felt-tip markers and crayons for this project.

With some practice your pupils may want to try their hand at making a filmstrip. For this you will need two slots on opposite sides of the bottle. They can create the filmstrips by either drawing a sequence on one long strip of cardboard or by taping together a series of individual hand-made slides. Clear transparent tape is used for this purpose.

HOW TO TEACH CREATIVE WRITING

Unlike mathematics or some exact science, creative writing requires more than just an accumulation of facts. Yet it can be taught successfully. In this chapter you will see how you can harness the imaginations of your pupils and help them express themselves on paper.

There are improvisations, story ideas, and picture clues that help pupils think for themselves and convey these thoughts to others through the printed word.

You will be helped to make use of magazine pictures, old manila files, and other found materials to stimulate the creative impulses of your pupils. There are competitive games that pit the creative energies of one team of pupils against those of another.

Self-starters and other launching ideas are found here for getting even the most reluctant writers to pick up their pencils and put some thoughts on paper.

Improvisations

AIM: *To help pupils improvise certain dramatic situations.*

Improvisation is something we do every day. When we cook without a recipe, make a bookcase without plans, or speak without a written speech we are "improvising." You can help your pupils write more creatively by giving them situations to work out as a group. While you, the teacher, present the problem to be worked out, the pupils provide the content of the drama (i.e., the characters and the situations) from their own experience. But they must work within the limits of the problem as set down by the teacher.

Even though improvisations or "improvs" are not written down, they can be used as a springboard for written expression.

Here are some situations or problems that you can ask a group of four or five students to improvise on:

1. You have come home late from a friend's house and your parents and older sister have been frantic looking for you.
2. Your mother finds your failing report card inside a jacket pocket. She is disappointed and angry.
3. Your best friend has invited you to go camping with his family. You must get your parents' permission.
4. Take a plot outline from a situation comedy that most of the children have seen on TV. Ask them to interpret the problem presented in their own way.

In order for the whole class to get anything out of this, they must participate in the evaluation. In evaluating the performers we do not judge them as "good" or "bad" but rather as "complete" or "incomplete." Did they solve the problem? Was it real? Did you believe them? These are some of the questions the audience will be expected to respond to. Watch the imaginative quality of pupils' written work improve after this.

Authors' File

AIM: *To stimulate pupils to write stories of their own.*

It's very hard for some children to write a story of their own without sufficient stimulation. The "authors' file" helps meet this need.

All you need for this activity is a batch of manila folders, some pictures taken from magazines, and a felt-tip marking pen. It's best if the pictures show some action. Paste the picture on one side of the manila folder; the right side works best. On the left side print five or six nouns and verbs that come to mind when you look at the picture for a minute or two. Do this on ten or twelve folders to start with.

The pupil selects a folder at random and takes it to his or her seat. The pupil then opens the folder and studies the picture. The next step is to write a story based on the picture. Somewhere in the story the pupil must use the words printed inside the folder.

If this is done well, the words will act as stimulants and idea-givers to the young author. Different pupils will come up with totally different stories. They will use the words differently.

You may want to point out to the class that it is not necessary for every word to be used in the story. If the words are carefully selected, they will serve to stimulate rather than hamper the pupils. Leave the title up to the pupils. With a very slow class you may find it easier to supply the title of the story as well as the group of words.

Capture the Captions

AIM: *To help pupils capture the essence of a situation in a few words.*

Help your pupils use their minds by focusing their attention on a single idea. Use an opaque projector to flash a cartoon on the screen after you have cut off the caption. Have the pupils write their own captions on a slip of paper. Turn off the projector and read some of the captions aloud. Redistribute the captions so that every pupil has a chance to read everyone else's caption. You will be amazed at the chuckles you will hear.

For homework, ask each pupil to clip three cartoons and cut off the caption. Tell them to paste each cartoon on a single sheet of filler paper. The next day pass these around the room. Have pupils write their own captions. Select the best ones and put them in a loose-leaf book. You will find that several pupils will bring in the same cartoon but the captions will be different.

Select a single cartoon for the bulletin board. Have the whole class write captions for this single cartoon. Select the six best captions and mount them under the posted cartoon.

Read the class an account of some local or national event from a recent issue of a newspaper or news magazine. Ask the class to write the headline. Have the pupils vote on the best headline for the story. Ask them why they liked the one they selected. Compare it with the one that was published. Review the qualities of a good headline.

Ask your pupils to bring in baby pictures of themselves or pictures of their pets. Mount these on colorful construction paper. Hold a contest for the best captions.

Look through your picture file. Mount pictures of action scenes. Ask your pupils to write picture titles. Help them see how to economize on words and yet convey the meaning.

Alphabet Books

AIM: *To provide pupils with a word puzzle for each letter of the alphabet.*

Children love to make up puzzles. What could be more fun than making up 26 puzzles on a single theme? For pupils in the lower grades you may want to select a social studies theme: "Our Community," or "The Farm." They then write short questions that can be answered by a letter of the alphabet. For example: A kind of crop. (<u>a</u>lfalfa.) A container for grain. (<u>b</u>ushel.) The Indians called it maize. (<u>c</u>orn.)

Older pupils can tackle a more sophisticated unit, like "Colonial Times."

Early document. (<u>A</u>rticles of Confederation.)
First ten amendments. (<u>B</u>ill of rights.)
Law-making branch. (<u>C</u>ongress.)
Paper declaring independence. (<u>D</u>eclaration of Independence.)

Of course, the going gets rough when pupils come to the letters q, x, and z. You may designate them FREE letters which means that they do not have to write a question for these letters. Or, you can call them BONUS puzzles which means that their answer can begin with any letter.

For a change of pace you can have intermediate level pupils make a nonsense book of rhymes for each letter of the alphabet. For this they must find two words that rhyme within a single sentence. For example:

I know an <u>a</u>nt that can't.
The <u>b</u>erry ate the cherry.
The <u>c</u>at wore a funny hat.
The <u>d</u>og got lost in the fog.

Again, caution the pupils not to worry too much about the x or z. They should be able to find a nonsense rhyme for these.

Word Ladders

AIM: *To introduce similes and metaphors with an emphasis on color words.*

Draw three simple ladders on the chalkboard. Ask the pupils to name their three favorite colors. Label the bottom rung of each ladder with the name of a different color.

Now, have the pupils recall various things that personify color. As you accept each color word, write it on another rung of the ladder. For example: if one ladder is labeled "yellow," some of the words or rungs might be lemon, butter, forsythia, daffodil, dandelion, sun, egg yolk, or pale gold.

Rewrite these word ladders on oaktag and display them around the room. Encourage your pupils to use them in their creative writing all year. For example, when discussing the use of the simile and the metaphor in writing, a pupil might say or write: "Her lemon yellow hair hung down." or "The buttercups were as yellow as the dandelion that grew in the fields a month before."

Point out to the pupils that in a simile you are making a comparison using the words "like" or "as." In a metaphor you are making a comparison without the use of these words.

Prepare a quiz in which pupils must write either a simile or metaphor for each of these color words:

snow	sky	clay
milk	ocean	sunset
dove	grass	heather
tomato	emerald	sand
apple	pearl	ice
fire	ruby	velvet
cherry	coal	sandpaper

Sentence Completion

AIM: *To give pupils a start in expressing a thought by completing a sentence fragment.*

People, like automobiles, need a start in the morning. For some of your reluctant writers try this energizer. Give the opening phrase of a "first" sentence. You literally put the words in their mouth—or on their paper.

Here are some provocative self-starters:

As I opened the door I saw a . . . .
If only my little sister would . . . .
I wish my mother . . . .
School is fun when . . . .
My happiest day was when . . . .
My dog loves to . . . .
The scariest time was when . . . .
If I could live anywhere in the world it would be . . . .
The day I won the lottery I . . . .
When I opened the abandoned trunk and found $5,000, ...
My brother's new car has . . . .
My mom makes me feel great when . . . .
It was one minute past midnight when . . . .
The day I fell out of a rocket ship I . . . .
If I had my own horse I would . . . .
Make believe you and I are going to the moon, and . . . .
Thing thing that makes me angry is when . . . .
I tried making new friends but . . . .
Most teachers think that . . . .
My friend asked me to do something that I knew would . . . .
My favorite TV show is . . . .

Flip-a-Story

AIM: *To help children create their own stories from three ideas.*

An old three-ring loose-leaf book or binder can supply you with an endless variety of story ideas. It is also great for individual or small group work. Cut three strips of oaktag and punch a hole in the top of each strip. The three strips together should equal the size of a piece of loose-leaf paper. One strip contains suggested characters for a story (WHO strips). The second strip contains situation ideas (WHAT strips). The third strip contains names of places (WHERE strips).

The child, group, or whole class creates his own story by choosing one strip from each of the three categories: Who, What, and Where. By putting just ten or 12 strips in each of the three categories, you will have the potential for dozens of different story lines.

Here are some ideas:

Who	What	Where
skier	an explosion	at school
angry mother	a TV show	downtown
butterfly	a race	in the furnace
lonely man	a party	in a store
teacher	a forest fire	in the park
football player	a vacation	on stage
sick cat	a hurricane	in the house
old dog	a desert	on campus
dying dinosaur	a volcano	on a farm
shark	a jail	in the car
Martian	an airport	in the sky
Karate expert	an ocean bottom	on the high seas
Wonder Woman	a skyscraper	uptown
lion tamer	a circus tent	in the country
Columbus	the Atlantic Ocean	at a hospital

Now, mix and match. For example: several flips may come up with a story about a *skier* who went to *a party at school.*

"You Don't Say!"

AIM: *To help pupils use their imagination in making up and writing conversations.*

Capitalize on your pupils' vivid imaginations by having them guess, from a picture, what two people are saying. Look through some magazines and find ten or 12 pictures of two people talking in a variety of situations. These can be from advertisements or news stories or fiction illustrations.

Mount these pictures on pieces of oaktag or construction paper. Break the class into groups of two or three and ask each group to write an imagined conversation between the people in the picture.

You will be amazed at the results! No two pupils will come up with the same conversation. Have all the pupils responding to the same picture read each other's papers. They will be surprised at the diversity of expression.

This is not the time to come down too heavily on the correct use of the quotation mark or punctuation. What is important is that the pupils feel free to express their thoughts and use their imagination. The mechanical details can come later.

Have the pupils responding to the same picture decide on the paper they like best. You can now give them some practice in reading aloud by having them act out the dialogue as it has been written by one of the pupils. As a variation of this you can have pairs of pupils work together as partners in writing conversations for a single picture.

Still another way is to let pupils act out their pictures before they actually write anything. In this way they can refine their ideas and dialog before putting a single word down on paper.

In a subsequent lesson you can illustrate the correct form for writing conversation. After some practice with this creative expression the pupils will see the rationale for using quotation marks and capital letters.

Opening Words

AIM: *To help pupils add variety to their beginning sentences.*

Review with your pupils their likes and dislikes in books found in the library. Many pupils will tell you that they read the opening paragraph of a fiction book in deciding whether or not they want to take it out.

Talk about the importance of opening remarks when listening to a speaker. Launch the class on a search for interesting first sentences from a variety of materials such as fiction, newspapers, magazine articles, advertisements. Suggest that pupils volunteer to read to the class an opening sentence that they like. Have the class secretary, if old enough, record a few of these on a large piece of newsprint. Post this chart in front of the room the following day and ask the pupils to write a single paragraph on the chart. Here are some likely candidates for the chart:

Just around the curve of the road I saw . . . .
The clock had just struck midnight when . . . .
Slowly the door closed as . . . .
It was a sticky, hot summer day in 1945 when . . . .
"Are you awake?" Mary anxiously asked her husband
        . . . .
About two blocks away from the site of the fire . . . .

At another time ask pupils to recall the first few words used in popular TV commercials. Point out that these are frequently attention-getting questions. Ask the pupils to write the copy for advertising a product of their own manufacture. Emphasize the important of the opening words. This can be an imaginary silly product or it can be something relating to ecology or health. Pupils love writing their own commercials. As a culminating activity have the class act out their commercial messages for the amusement or edification of a neighboring class. The other class can vote on the one they like the best.

A New Twist

AIM: *To help pupils write their own ending to a story.*

Pupils frequently ask, "How did it all turn out?" In this exercise each pupil has the story turn out a different way, his or her own way. Read aloud a suitable folk tale or piece of current juvenile fiction. Stop reading just before the story ends. Encourage your class to write their own ending to the story. Caution them not to write the kind of ending the author had in mind but rather the kind of ending they have in mind.

After the class has had a chance to do this, read aloud the author's conclusion to the story. Now ask volunteers to read their ending to the story. Lead a discussion on which of the several endings was the most satisfying. Which was the most likely to occur in real life? Why?

Take advantage of the class' current interest in science fiction or biography. Here they will have a change of pace between fancy and factual endings.

For additional practice, ditto a situation, leaving sufficient space on ruled lines for the pupil's answer. Post on the class bulletin board the most imaginative endings.

Once the class has gotten the swing of doing this you can amuse and delight them by encouraging them to write endings with a new twist for each of these well-known stories:

Cinderella
Sleeping Beauty
The Headless Horseman
Superman
Joseph and his brothers
Noah and the Ark

"If" Stories

AIM: *To give pupils experience in conjecturing about situations.*

Daydreaming can become a legitimate activity in your classroom. Encourage your children to think about what would happen "if." For example, what would you do:

If you were a lost puppy?
If you were a red balloon and your string broke?
If you won $100,000 in a contest?
If your family moved to Hawaii?
If you became a doctor?
If school were kept open during the summer?
If you were a wild pony?
If you could fly?

Encourage your pupils to think about one of these situations for a moment before starting to write. After the pupils have had a chance to write a brief story, ask the class to group themselves according to the "if" story they selected. Give each group a chance to hear every story in their group. Then ask each group to choose one author to read his or her selection for the whole class.

Hand out drawing paper and have the pupils illustrate their stories.

In Other Words

AIM: *To help pupils turn commonplace expressions into more elegant language.*

This game capitalizes on your pupils' love of big words. It also helps them enjoy a sense of humor. When someone uses "fancy" language at the expense of clarity, the class will laugh. It will help your children to learn that words, like clothes, must suit the occasion.

The teacher will need a list of proverbs, mottos, and idiomatic expressions, and several slips of paper. Write the expression, a different one on each slip of paper, and fold it in half. Give one to each pupil playing the game. Within a given time, the pupil must rewrite the expression on his paper. Suggest that the pupils capture the essential meaning but cloak the expression in such formal language that it will be hard to decipher.

Select teams and have the captain of each team select a reader. After he reads from his slip of paper, the other team must state what proverb or other common expression he started with.

For example, the reader may state: "Do not lament about the overturn of a vessel containing bovine fluid." A bright team member from the opposing team might come up with: "Don't cry over spilt milk." It would then be his turn to read his translation of a popular expression.

Here's a good one. See if you can figure it out. "Refrain from transversing a structure erected over a river prior to the time of your arrival."

Remember, you write the common expression; the pupils come up with the longer, more formal translation. In addition to proverbs you can write song titles, names of TV programs, etc.

Headline News

AIM: *To write a story when given just the newspaper headline.*

Point out to the class that newspaper stories are written first and then the headlines are made up for them. For this exercise the reverse will be followed. You will give the class a provocative headline and they will be asked to write a newspaper story that is likely to have such a headline.

You can begin by recording on the chalkboard interesting newspaper headlines that the children have brought to school. Each pupil selects a headline that interests him and then creates a story supporting it. Some intriguing headlines are:

Building Collapses
$10,000 Found in Trash Can
Longest Baseball Game on Record

Mercury Breaks Summer Record
Gas Shortage Seen
Dog Rescues Handicapped Girl

After the pupils write their stories, have them read them to the class. Compare these to the actual news accounts and compare the style.

Point out that many news articles contain the essential information in the lead paragraph. Help the pupils acquire this skill by rewriting some of their stories.

Add another dimension to this story-writing experience by setting up a tape recorder and having the pupils play the role of a TV or radio newscaster. After the stories have been read aloud, play back the tape. Watch the faces of the pupil-newscasters as they hear their own voices!

Point out to the class that a different style is needed for writing news stories for radio or TV than for writing a similar story in a newspaper. Ask the pupils why they think this is so. For homework ask the class to watch a TV newscaster give the six o'clock news. Then read the same story as reported in the daily paper.

Off the Wall

AIM: *To capitalize on the urge to write graffiti.*

Archeologists tell us that graffiti was found on the walls unearthed in the ruins of ancient Pompei. So obviously graffiti has been around a long time. But don't tell that to your school custodian! Here is something that children and custodians love.

Cover a section of wall in the classroom with brown wrapping paper marked into bricks, and let the pupils write graffiti in each brick. The class can also create their own collection of graffiti in book form.

Here are some random items we have seen:

Bakers make a lot of dough.
Dopes smoke dope.
A bird in the hand is an unhappy bird.
Operations are a real pain.
If you can read this, you don't need glasses.
My grade on the Middle East test was a Dead C.
Pike's Peak or bust.
You are what you eat. Try blubber.

Adding Color to Writing

AIM: *To help pupils write with vivid language.*

List on the chalkboard words that show emotional expressions, such as laughing, crying, frowning. Have several pupils use these words in sentences such as these:

The man is laughing.
The boy is crying.
She was frowning.

Then have other pupils describe the expression without using the key word, as for instance:

The man's eyes twinkled.
Tears are coming down the boy's face.
She looked angry.

Divide the class into two teams and hold a competition in the use of this technique.

For variety, write on the chalkboard a simple sentence such as "The man opened the door."

Then ask the class to write this so that it tells more about what happened or how the man felt. Elicit sentences such as:

The man threw open the door.
The man stomped across the room and angrily threw open the door.

Discuss these sentences with the class, helping the pupils to recognize that details, descriptive phrases, and descriptive words give a clearer picture or sharper impression of what is meant.

Talk about the role of vivid language in writing and the manner in which such language affects a reader. Then show slides of interesting scenes and objects and have various pupils give two or three descriptive sentences concerning the picture. Compare several of the samples offered and let the pupils decide which is the most vivid description.

—12—

PHYSICAL EDUCATION GAMES

Your physical education program must serve all of your pupils—normal, gifted, handicapped, poorly coordinated, slow learning, and All-American. Physical activity games and exercise are essential to them all. In this chapter you will find new ideas to use in the gym, school yard, classroom, and during lunch recess time.

A greater effort is being made to have "lifetime sports" activities taught in the schools. The reason is simple. If an individual learns basic skills in sports activities he or she can continue to pursue and enjoy throughout life, continued physical activity will become an important and natural part of the lifestyle. That is why we have incorporated in this chapter such games as classroom bowling and hoop ball. Because it is essential that young people learn how to play and use this "free" time in a positive way we have included activities like "Playground Quickies" and "Jug Ball."

The physical education ideas you find here will also develop a strong self-concept in all your pupils because they will be able to succeed and they will be competing against themselves.

Indoor Hit-Pin Ball

AIM: *To provide a softball type game using an indoor area.*

Equipment needed:

4 large detergent bottles or Indian clubs to mark home, first, second, and third bases;
1 large utility or basketball;
1 empty carton or roll-out basketball hoop.

Organize two teams, A and B. (See Figure 12-1.) Team A is lined up at home plate. Team B is scattered in the field with players at each base. Members of each team are numbered. Fielder #1 is responsible for making the out when the opposing team's #1 player is up. Fielder #2 makes the out when player #2 is up, and so on.

The "up" player stands at home plate, holds the ball in his hands, hits it anywhere in the gym except behind home plate, and runs all the bases.

Fielders field the ball and pass it to the fielder responsible for making the out. The out is made if the appropriate fielder makes a basket or carton before the runner gets home. The runner must knock down the pins with his hands as he rounds each base. He may NOT kick the bases over.

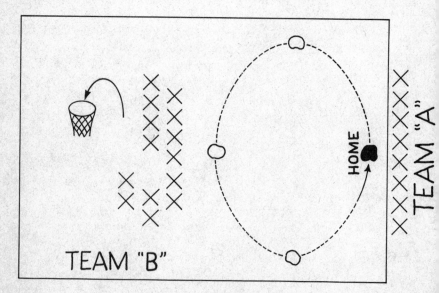

Figure 12-1

One point is scored for each successful run. Sides may be changed after every player at home plate has had a turn or after a designated number of outs have been made.

A restraining line may be drawn around the basketball standard so basket making will be more difficult if advanced ability warrants it.

Remember—a regular hoop can be used or a "basket" can be scored by getting the ball into the carton.

Hop-Along Skip-Along

AIM: *To give young children practice in hopping and skipping.*

The only material you need for this energizer is one or two rolls of black electrician's tape. An inexpensive substitute is black photographer's tape which resembles masking tape.

Make a floor diagram similar to the one in Figure 12-2.

Beginning with the X, the pupil steps onto the first footprint with his or her right foot and hops from box to box. Upon reaching the third box, the child steps onto the next print and repeats the movement with the left foot. The final portion of the exercise is completed by jumping from one side of the center line to the other, taking off and landing with both feet at once as shown in the diagram.

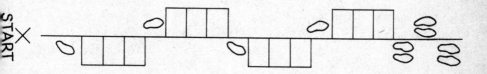

Figure 12-2

You can teach the class to skip by making a similar diagram with just one box alternating on each side of the line (Figure 12-3). The pupil starts at the X, takes a step with the right foot onto the first footprint, then hops into the box. The next step must be a step—not a leap—onto the next footprint, followed by a hop into the box. This is continued to the end of the diagram.

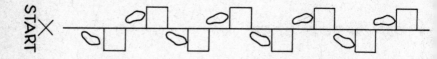

Figure 12-3

Classroom Bowling

AIM: *To develop fundamental bowling skills.*

You can give your pupils pointers in bowling without the use of a professional alley or bowling balls. Your pupils will acquire sound habits that will help them when they go to the regular bowling alley.

Use quart milk cartons that have been rinsed clean. Softballs or rubber balls of that size make good bowling balls for your purpose. At first try "3-3 Bowling." Instead of ten pins, use three pins and three chances for each frame. Set the milk cartons on spots that are six inches apart in the form of an equilateral triangle.

If your pupil is right handed, encourage him or her to aim for the 1-3 pocket. The ball should hit both these pins as it is rolled between them, and the head pin, number 1, should be deflected to knock down the number 2 pin.

The pupil gets three tries. The pins are set back up only after all three are knocked down. The score is the total number of pins knocked down in that frame. For example, a child could score anywhere from zero to nine points in one turn. Five turns makes a good game.

Encourage your pupils to work in pairs, with one person scoring while the other person returns the ball and sets up the pins.

A variation is to have groups of four. One person rolls, one keeps score, the third sets pins, and the fourth checks the scorekeeper. Members of the group rotate the position.

As your pupils gain confidence and skill, move them up to these leadup games or modified games:

Bowlite Bowling
Indian Club or Rubber Pin Bowling
King-Pin Bowling
Lawn Bowls
Bowl Spot Ball

Simple Movement

AIM: *To learn basic elements of movement education.*

Take your class to an empty room or a quiet corner of the gym. Start with a short session of ten or fifteen minutes and steadily increase the time spent. This can be done with one or two children, a group, or even the whole class. It works best with a small group. Perhaps you can take a group from your class and another class while the other teacher supervises the bulk of the children in the school yard.

Begin with balancing activities. Have the pupils stand on the left foot, bend the right leg back at the knee, hold the leg in the right hand, and then slowly raise the left arm straight out and up. The pupils should hold this position as long as possible. Train them to stare at a spot on the wall as they remain in this position. This aids their ability to concentrate. When tired, the pupil brings the left arm down slowly to the side and slowly lowers the leg.

Repeat this exercise, using the opposite side of the body. Remind the pupils not to let the arm or foot drop but to bring each back down slowly and carefully.

A more advanced balance position of this type is to bend forward when in full position and hold while pressing foot into the hand. Later they can try the balance beam.

Have your pupils try the anti-gravity walk. This will improve their circulations and straighten their backs. It is really quite simple—and will help the teacher improve her circulation as well. Have the children stand with their feet about six inches apart. Tell them to bend over and place the palms of their hands on the floor in front of their feet. It is important that their buttocks be as high up in the air as possible for this exercise. Their heads are now lower than their hips. Tell them to begin to "walk" on their hands and feet. This is harder than it seems. Start them walking in a straight line. Later they can make turns and walk in a circle.

Hoop Ball

AIM: *To develop motor coordination.*

This is a fun game that can be played indoors or out. All you need are two large plastic hoops (similar to the old "hula hoops") and two rubber balls.

Divide the class into two teams. Make sure each team has an odd number of players. The teams form two lines facing one another about six feet apart. Assume that one team is called Team A and the other is called Team B. It is important that you line the players up with team members alternating.

One line might look like this:

A B A B A B A B A B A B A B A

You notice that the first and last player on this line is from Team A. The facing line will have the first and last player from Team B, thus evening things out.

Hand the hoops to two players at diagonal ends and the balls to those at the other diagonal ends. At your signal the hoops are rolled down the line, and each player with a ball tries to throw it through either moving hoop to a teammate across the aisle.

The team members at the end continue rolling the hoops back and forth and each team attempts to move the ball along. A point is scored every time a ball goes through a hoop.

When the ball reaches one end, the players reverse the route. To insure good hoop rolls, deduct a point for every bad roll. A bad roll is when the hoop doesn't make it from end to end without touching someone or falling down. The team with the most points at the end wins.

Playground Quickies

AIM: *To provide simple games for pupils to play after lunch.*

Penny tag

The player chosen to be IT is given a penny. Holding his hands behind his back, he hides the penny in one hand. Then he holds both fists in front of him. All the other players start the game three giant steps away. IT calls out to an opponent who tries to guess which hand has the penny. If he guesses correctly, he can take another step away from IT. If he guesses incorrectly, IT takes a giant step towards him. This continues until someone is caught and becomes the new IT.

Three-legged race

Racing partners stand side by side, facing the same direction. The left leg of one partner is secured to the right leg of the other. Use flimsy bindings such as Scotch tape or thin string. This will require the partners to race very carefully, and they are less likely to hurt themselves on a hard surfaced school yard.

Ape

Explain that to ape someone is to mimic him. Players take turns being the leader. Everyone tries to ape or mimic exactly what the leader does. He may decide to be a machine (like a computer), or a ferocious animal, or he may decide to create some movements that are new. Players who do not do exactly what the leader does must drop out. It is important to select as the first leader someone who can get the game off to a good start.

Throw and Run

AIM: *To improve your class' ability to throw a ball.*

Equipment:

1 beanbag or small rubber ball.
3 flags or Indian clubs to mark distances in the outfield.
1 home plate marker. (See Figure 12-4).

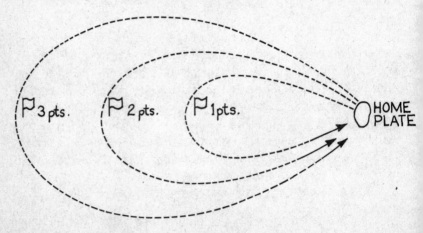

Figure 12-4

Divide your class into two even teams. Team A has one player up at a time. Team B has a catcher positioned at home plate and the other players scattered in the field.

Whoever is up at home plate throws the ball or beanbag anywhere in the field. Depending on the distance of his throw he decides which flag he will try to run around and get back home before the ball is fielded and thrown to the catcher. Safely circling the first flag earns him one point; the second, two points; the third, three points.

The player runs only once until every player has had a turn. Outs occur when a fly ball is thrown and when the ball beats a runner home. Sides may be changed after an entire team has had a turn or when a team has three outs.

Jug Ball

AIM: *To provide catching skills with homemade equipment.*

A great piece of "found material" for physical education is the plastic milk or bleach jug. Don't throw yours away, and encourage your pupils to bring in their empty jugs from home.

Just cut the bottom with a razor blade or utility knife. There is a line about one inch from the bottom that can be used as a guide for an even cut. Don't let the pupils do the cutting—and keep your razor blade or knife in a safe place. The finished scoop, and it is finished when you make the cut and throw away the bottom, is ideal for any throwing and catching game.

Use the scoops for indoor or outdoor wiffle ball, wiffle baseball, and Lacrosse. Best of all are the games your pupils will invent for the scoops during free play time.

The jugs can be stored easily. They stack easily on top of each other. A holder can be made from a broom handle. Be sure to use a soft rubber ball; a sponge ball will work well. If a jug tears or is ruined it is easily replaced with another.

You can use whole, uncut jugs for other games, also. Without any cutting they can be used as markers for games in the gym or on Field Day. Just add water or sand and replace the cap. This added weight will stabilize them. A little yellow or red paint will make them visible from quite a distance.

We have seen one group of school yard kids invent their own version of volley ball, using a volley ball net and court, and with every player using a jug scoop as a combination bat and catching scoop. Other children have come up with a form of Jai Alai using the plastic jugs. We're sure your pupils will be equally inventive.

Batting Over the Line

AIM: *To provide practice in batting.*

This activity may be played by two teams with five players or less. The batting team furnishes its own pitcher and catcher. Batters have a batting order. Players rotate pitcher, catcher, batter. The batter tries to hit the ball over an imaginary line drawn between the second and third bases and into fair territory. When a batter hits the ball, he runs the bases as far as possible before the ball is fielded and thrown back over the line between second and third. This action stops the runner on the last base touched. The runner then returns to the batting bench.

This can be varied. The batter hits the ball to any number of players placed anywhere in the playing area. Next, the batter places the bat on the ground, permitting the fielder to roll the ball at the bat. If the ball strikes the bat, the batter must catch the ball in the air. If the batter misses the ball, he is out. The fielder who rolled the ball becomes the batter. Any player in the field who catches a fly ball also becomes the batter.

Still another variation is called "Three Flys." Here the game is played in the same way except that the fielder must catch three fly balls to become the batter.

Double Basketball Drill

AIM: *To emphasize catching and passing skills in basketball.*

Have your pupils make a circle with eight or nine players. More than one circle can be formed. A leader is selected for the center of each circle. The leader and pupil Number 1 each have a ball. At the command of "Go" by the leader, the balls are passed as follows:

Center to Number 2.
Number 1 to Center.
Center to Number 3.
Number 2 to Center, etc.

When all the participants have passed and received the ball, the group rotates until each pupil has had a chance at center.

As a variation, use different passes, such as bounce passes, etc. The ball is not to be passed until the Center player passes his ball.

Teaching cues:

Start with short passes thrown at one-quarter speed.
Emphasize the give of elbows, hands, and arms.
Keep your eye on the ball at all times.
Spread, curve, and relax the fingers.
Advance in your movement to meet the ball.
The ball is stopped in its flight with the fingers, not in the palm of the hand.

Modified Softball

AIM: *To become acquainted with the rules of softball.*

Here are three modifications of softball that you can use with your class. The first is called "Three-Pitch Softball."

The regular softball rules are used with these modifications:

1. Twelve to fifteen players on a side.
2. Batting team uses its own pitcher.
3. Batter receives a maximum of three pitches.
4. Batter is out if batted ball hits or is fielded by the pitcher.
5. Bunting is not permitted.
6. Stealing bases or taking a lead off base is not permitted.
7. Two outs retire a side.
8. Each batter is allowed only one swing.

"Twelve-Player Softball" has four teams of three pupils each. One team is at bat; the second team plays the pitcher, catcher and shortstop position; the third team plays first, second, and third base; and the fourth team plays the outfield. The batting team must maintain a regular batting order. Each base runner must reach home for his turn at bat or be declared out. Three outs retire the side, which then takes over the outfield. The other teams each move up.

"All or Nothing at All" uses the regular softball rules with these exceptions: No put out may be made at second or third base. Once past first base, the batter must run all the way around to home. Outs are made by (1) catching a fly; (2) throwing ball to first base before the runner arrives; (3) throwing ball to first, second, and third base and to home before the runner arrives.

Tug-of-War

AIM: *To provide vigorous activity that emphasizes group effort.*

We are going to describe a traditional form of tug-of-war and several variations. This can be played almost anywhere with any even-numbered group of players from two to one hundred. This game pits one group against another, at opposing ends of a rope.

Start with the center of the rope placed over a clearly marked dividing line on the floor. The center of the rope can be marked with electrician's tape. Two other pieces of tape are placed on the rope, at equal distances from the center. The object is to pull this predetermined length of the opposing team's half of the rope across the center line. Six feet is a good length.

You can vary the basic game by one-hand, sitting, kneeling, over-the shoulder, and face-the-rear tugging.

Snake tug-of-war keeps the rope on the floor. Each contestant places a foot on the rope and pulls with that foot. The hardest part of this contest is to avoid laughing.

Circle tug-of-war ties the rope ends together. A circle is formed that is divided by the center floor-line. Each team controls its half of the circle. This places the teams in a face-to-face confrontation. The first team to get both ends of the opposing team's half circle across the center line wins.

Your class will help you think of other variations. Just be on the lookout for the youngster who seems to be getting squeezed by his or her classmates.

—13—

GUIDANCE AND CAREER EDUCATION ACTIVITIES

We in the schools have had to assume greater responsibilities in the area of child guidance and career education. These goals are best achieved when they are integrated into the general curriculum rather than taught in isolation. In this chapter, you will have illustrated for you 14 different ways to help your pupils grow as individuals and grow in the area of career awareness.

Did you ever want to help your pupils develop greater self-confidence or self-control? Try the self-concept center ideas and see the glow in the faces of your pupils. Want to do some significant role-playing without getting clinical? Try "Roles people play." How about some lively "Brain Teasers" with answers that some pupil with a fragile ego can test his or her classmates with?

Are you tired of the sex stereotyping you find in school books, TV series, and advertising? Join your pupils in some of the activities described in the next few pages that help erase rigid male-female barriers. You'll want to try these brain teasers and games as soon as you read them.

Reward Punch

AIM: *To provide pupils with a tangible reward system.*

Everyone likes to be rewarded. Medals, certificates, letters of commendation and other tangible rewards are handed out every day in the adult world. For some reason, in schools we usually wait until graduation before we distribute any tangible rewards. Why not change this in your classroom? All you need is a hand punch, the kind that you use to make round holes in loose-leaf paper, and a package of 3″ × 5″ cards.

Have each pupil write his or her name in large letters on the unruled side of the card. On the ruled side, have the pupils number from 1 through 25. Remind pupils to keep their cards in their desks and to have them available all the time.

Discuss with your class the kinds of behaviors and actions that will earn a "reward punch." These might include marked improvement in a skill or conduct, helpful service, special consideration of another person, etc. Explain, too, that after 25 punches a special prize will be awarded.

Since there is no extrinsic value in the hole punch itself, you are not bribing your pupils to improve. Children do appreciate some immediate gratification for positive things they do and you are providing that. Watch the hard-to-reach pupils grin when you punch their card!

A group guidance experience can be shared when you ask the class to help you decide whether a particular action is deserving of a "reward punch."

Up or Down

AIM: *To help pupils recognize feelings in others and themselves.*

There are some days when everything looks miserable, and, fortunately, many days when things are just fine. As adults we recognize this and deal with it. Children sometimes are troubled when they don't feel like smiling or when they are feeling down.

Very often this feeling can change when someone does something nice for you.

Try this simple badge technique and watch the sun come out in your class. All you need is some drawing paper, crayons, scissors, and a supply of round plastic lids, such as the kind that come with coffee cans or non-dairy topping. Ask your pupils to trace two circles and cut them out to fit both sides of the plastic lid. On one circle they should draw a happy face (similar to those on the "have a nice day" stickers) and on the other side a sad face (with the corners of the mouth turned down).

If your pupils have trouble getting the paper circles to adhere to the plastic, try strips of cellophane tape along the edge. Carefully make a hole near the top and thread a colorful lanyard strip through each lid so that when the lanyard is placed over the head, the lid hangs like a medallion.

Explain to the class that people do not always feel like smiling. As members of the class everyone is going to do something a little extra for the person wearing a "down" or sad face. Discuss some simple, subtle things that pupils can do for one another: choosing the "down" pupil as a partner, sharing a game, complimenting an article of clothing, etc.

You will be fascinated at the unique ways in which UP pupils go out of their way to help DOWN pupils. When someone who is down feels better, he or she turns his or her lid around. You will even find "downers" helping other "downers." Watch when a down side is turned around—it's like catching a glimpse of a shooting star.

Circle of Praise

AIM: *To build pupils' sense of worth and self-esteem.*

This is based on the "I'm OK, you're OK" philosophy, which says, in part, everyone needs to give and get some praise.

Divide your class into three circles. Give each pupil a number of 3″ × 5″ cards equal to the number of people in the circle. Ask each pupil to write down one thing he or she likes about *each* member of the circle. Statements can be superficial or deep. Leave it up to the writer. For example; "I like your jeans" or "I like the way you treat people." It would be best to leave the statements unsigned. In some situations you may want to have the pupils sign their cards. You'll have to play that by ear.

Encourage your pupils to follow two simple rules:

1. The statements must not be longer than ten words.
2. The statements must be truthful.

The moment of truth comes when the statements are handed out to the subjects written about. Pupils are then invited to share any of the comments they received by reading them or by arranging them in a flip book. (A flip book is merely a 3″ × 5″ card cover stapled to the collection of cards received.)

You as the teacher should remain aware of which children receive the cards most eagerly or for whom the praise is especially needed. Watch them glow and grow under the influence of your "Circle of Praise."

Interviews

AIM: *To help pupils recognize people in their environment from life clues.*

Here is a game that upper graders love to play. We call it "Interviews." It involves your pupils with adults in the community and appeals to their sense of shrewd guessing and curiosity.

Discuss interviews and read newspaper examples aloud. Talk about favorite TV talk shows and how the host draws out the guest.

Together with your pupils draw up a list of people in the

community who might consent to an interview with one member of the class. For example: school crossing guard, policeman, PTA president, principal, religious leader, storekeeper, fire captain, baker, etc. Place the agreed-upon names in a box. Each child draws one name. If they want to switch among themselves, it's OK, if agreeable to both parties.

Discuss what you want to know about each person and decide on general categories: family background, birthplace, schooling, hobbies. Remind pupils to make an appointment first. After two weeks' time, the pupils bring their notes to class and the game begins. One at a time the pupil-interviewer gets up and gives us "clues" based on the categories. Ten guesses are allowed. A scorekeeper determines which subjects were the hardest to guess. Pupils analyze the techniques used by the pupil-interviewers.

The pupils usually leave this game with renewed respect for the community members interviewed. They also take away a deeper understanding of the varying life styles around them.

Challenge Cards

AIM: *To build up a shattered ego with the use of brain teasers.*

Since everyone likes to know the answer to something that puzzles others we like to keep on hand a supply of "Challenge Cards." These are $3'' \times 5''$ index cards with a brain teaser on one side and the answer on the reverse side. We usually hand out two or three of these cards to some pupil who looks as though he is having a bad day. He or she can then go around the room and "challenge" someone else to solve the brain teaser. If the challenger succeeds, he or she gains possession of the card for the day.

Here are some favorite brain teasers you can use:

1. Name the month or months with   All 12 months
    28 days.   have 28 days.

2. How many states being with the   Eight
   letter "M"?

3. Arrange the digits 1,2,3,4,5,6,7 $15+36+47+2=100$
   so that they will add up to 100.

4. A pen and a pencil cost $1.10, the   The pen cost $1.05
   pen costing $1.00 more than the   and the pencil cost
   pencil. What was the cost of each?   five cents.

5. If six coins total 48 cents, the
   six coins will consist of   one quarter
   _____ quarters   two dimes
   _____ dimes   no nickels
   _____ nickels   three pennies
   _____ pennies

6. A tree doubled in height every   19 years, since it
   year until it reached its full   doubled its height
   height in 20 years. How many   every year.
   years did it take this tree to
   reach half its full height?

7. How can you write the number 100,
   using six nines?

$$99 \frac{99}{99}$$

Getting Personal

AIM: *To help pupils recognize their own identity.*

This game is sometimes called "Who Am I?" Pupils need to see their own identity as individuals and this game helps. Give each pupil the assignment of describing himself or herself in five short statements. After hearing all five, the other pupils in the class may or may not be able to guess the author of the five statements. For example:

WHO AM I?

1. I am one of five children.
2. My house is near the hospital.
3. I came to this school in the third grade.
4. I like reading books about horses.
5. My desk is near the window.

Besides having fun with this activity, the pupils get a great deal out of it by thinking about their own identity. Remind pupils that each statement must be about another area of their life. They could not, for example, take five statements to describe where they sit in the room. Encourage them to include these areas in writing statements: family, home, school, hobbies, class activities, awards, favorite things.

Here is another one to get you going:

1. I want to become a scientist.
2. My mother works at Sears.
3. I am on the Service Squad.
4. I love fried chicken.
5. My dog recently had puppies.

Self-Concept Center

AIM: *To help enhance pupils' concepts of themselves.*

Here are some guessing games that help pupils see that they are different from everyone else while still sharing certain similarities.

1. Appoint three pupils who are good with crayons to assist you for this one. Have the rest of the class lie on the floor and trace around them on wrapping paper. Have the pupils paint the figures to correspond with clothing they are wearing. Wait a week and then

have small groups of pupils display their finished likenesses around the room. The rest of the group guesses which shape is which child.

2. Have pupils paint and draw pictures of themselves in a family situation. Accept each child's picture, and do not prod for more finished work that may be beyond the child's ability. Ask pupils to tell what is taking place in each picture.

3. Pair pupils off in groups of two. Ask them to stare at one another and write a description similar to the kind the FBI posts in its "wanted" descriptions found in the Post Office. Next, have them write a more detailed description such as a novelist might write. When each pair has finished they exchange with the rest of the class, and that is where the fun begins. At the start the teacher assigns a code number to each paper. She notes this number next to her class roster. After numbered sketches are read aloud, the rest of the class guesses as to who is being described. Only the teacher knows for sure.

4. Use a tape recorder to have pupils read aloud a previously written class commercial for a fictitious home product. This can be humorous or serious. The object of the game is for the class to listen to each unidentified voice and decide who is speaking. Frequently the speaker will not recognize his or her own voice.

New Child in Class

AIM: *To find ways to facilitate a new child's adjustment to class.*

In our mobile society teachers are constantly absorbing "new" pupils into class after the start of school. Here are things you can do to make the adjustment smoother.

1. "Hello" booklets help acquaint the new pupils with the rest of the class. It is made up of the names, addresses, phone numbers, and hobbies of each pupil in the class.

2. After the child fills out his or her own card you will have a hint as where to seat the new pupil.

3. Prepare home-school maps on a rexograph master. Get input from your pupils and clearly indicate home locations in relation to the school and to each other. Bus routes and transportation methods between various locations can be penciled in during a map study lesson. Neighborhood centers, Y's, and other places of interest should be included.

4. Utilize older siblings. Ask help from older brothers and sisters in planning new ways to make new, younger students feel at home in the school. One way is to match up a big sibling with one or more younger students who live near each other or who are in the same homeroom. Older siblings can also be used as peer counselors in the school. The older siblings should be prepared to listen well and talk straight to the children who come to them for advice.

5. Involve parents. To add both to the new child's sense of belonging and to your sense of the child, encourage his or her parents to participate in some way in school activities. One way is to initiate an international food luncheon that parents, including those of the new pupil, can participate in.

Roles People Play

AIM: *To explore the various roles people play within an institution.*

Give each child a piece of paper that you have labeled "PLANE TICKET." Most of the pupils should receive a single ticket that has dittoed on it this statement: "On the plane you are free to be anyone you want." Explain that during this game, pupils must forget the real world and its restrictions.

Give three or four pupils a single restricted ticket, crayoned another color, that has this statement: "On the plane you are the pilot." Have the pupils imagine that they are on a jet plane high above the Atlantic Ocean. On this plane there are five roles: pilot, stewardess, navigator, passenger, and plainclothes policeman. Ask the pupils to choose which they want to be. Encourage the pupils to act out the roles they choose.

Act out emotional situations that may occur on a large jet plane. For example, a bomb threat is overheard, a woman gives birth to a baby, a considerable quantity of fuel has been lost, a severe storm approaches, etc. Ask all those playing pilot to meet and discuss why they chose that activity, while those choosing other roles also meet and exchange ideas on their choices. Ask each group to report to the class their reasons for selecting a particular role.

Discuss at another time:

1. What similarities are there between the roles on this plane and the roles people play in a school, business, club, church, city?
2. What did it feel like to be the pilot, knowing that the final decisions had to be yours?
3. Why would you never want to be the captain or pilot? (if youngsters give this response)
4. Does everyone want to play pilot at one time or another?

Present and Future

AIM: *To provide pupils with an opporunity to display their individuality.*

Select a few pupils to be the class journalists. They have the responsibility of interviewing members of the class to find out some of their favorite things. Have the pupils make a bulletin board display on the order of the one shown here. (Every few days, different pupils can be featured.)

MY FAVORITE THINGS

James	Roger	Louisa
punchball	skateboards	reading
mopeds	science	piano
recess	model cars	boating
pecan pie	pizza	tennis
Superman	TV	telephone

The class then gazes into an imaginary crystal ball and predicts what the future will hold for each pupil. These prophecies are based on present interests and that is how the game gets its name, Present and Future. The crystal-gazing may be humorous or quite serious. It should be based on facts uncovered in the interviewing.

Career Quiz

AIM: *To provide pupils with an awareness of the world of work.*

Contact your local chamber of commerce to find out which businessmen are available to talk to small groups during the working day or just before it. When you contact these speakers you will find that many of them would like to stop by early in the morning or around lunch time.

Prepare your class for their visit. Invite some of them for breakfast or a light lunch. Help structure the class visit by thinking ahead of time of questions your pupils could ask the visitor. Try to get speakers from different career areas. Don't confine your source to the chamber of commerce. Contact parents, unions, friends, and professional associations. Try to have broad career areas represented, such as health careers, the legal profession, service industries, crafts, cultural endeavors, office workers, mechanical trades, etc.

Give each speaker a few minutes to make any kind of presentation he or she wishes. Then follow up with a career quiz panel of five pupils. Let them prepare broad questions ahead of the visit. They may then follow with more detailed, spontaneous questions that occur to them while the speaker is making his presentation or answering the prepared questions. Have one panel member act as chairman. This should rotate from visitor to visitor. Here are some good prepared questions:

1. What personal characteristics are needed for your job?
2. What are your other job experiences, training, education?
3. What are the advantages and disadvantages of your work?
4. Where does one begin your kind of work?
5. Where can it lead?
6. Will there be a need for your kind of work in 15 years?

This career quiz will impress your visitor and save much of his or her time. If, of course, one or more of these questions were anticipated by the speaker, the panel member should ask another question or pass to another pupil.

Occupation Search

AIM: *To integrate career education into your existing curriculum.*

You can help your pupils see the need for the subjects they are studying when they experience activities related to the working world. Try some of these energizers:

1. Have pupils bring in the Sunday paper's want ads. Help them understand the abbreviations and other code words. Explain the kinds of training needed by job applicants. Point out the methods of responding: phone, walk-in, post office box.
2. Use old yellow page directories. Encourage pupils to cut out occupations that appeal to them. Write some basic occupations on the chalkboard and have pupils locate businesses that would employ each kind of worker.

3. Write a job description for jobs performed in the classroom, such as librarian, messenger, book clerk, etc. Have pupils draw up an application blank for each job. Check for completeness and make duplicate copies on a spirit copier. Give pupils practice in filling out a job application correctly and neatly.

4. After a field trip, instead of the usual composition, ask pupils to make a list of all the kinds of jobs they saw performed, starting with the bus driver. Have them comment on the quality of service they saw performed in each job. For example, zoo keepers, tour guides, receptionists, plant managers, ticket collectors, public relations personnel.

5. Establish a classroom newspaper. Write job descriptions for editors, reporters, illustrators, photographers, printers, distributors, business managers, ad takers.

6. Have pupils fill out deposit slips and checks and then do related math problems.

7. Role-play storekeeper and buy and sell items brought from home. Write advertising copy for each item.

8. Have pupils prepare a weekly budget. "Give" them an imaginary sum of money each Friday. Have them budget this weekly allowance and keep track of where the money went on the following Thursday.

This occupation search will make your pupils increasingly aware of the kinds of jobs they see performed around them and the kinds of skills that workers in each field must possess.

Stamping Out Sex Stereotyping

AIM: *To make your pupils aware of the ways in which society still discriminates against one sex in one way or another.*

This is not a brain teaser but rather a brain alert to increase your pupils' awareness of sex stereotyping. Have them help you find ways, subtle and otherwise, in which the world around them shows a bias toward one sex or the other. Here are a few starters.

1. Analyze the appeals of the ads in a general magazine such as: *TV Guide, Time, Newsweek, Reader's Digest.* Now contrast that with the ads in magazines like *Good Housekeeping* or *Popular Science.*

2. Distribute some basal readers that are the oldest ones available in your school. Help pupils count the numbers of male main characters and female main characters. Is either sex "put down" in any way? Pupils of which sex seem to be having the most fun?

3. Discuss some popular TV situation comedy. Help pupils look critically at the portrayal of family members.

4. Design a flag or banner as a symbol for people's rights in a non-sexist society.

5. Ask pupils to describe a children's book they read in which the father's role and the mother's role were portrayed fairly.

6. Listen to popular music on the radio. How are men and women depicted by writers of song lyrics?

7. Visit the toy department of a local store and draw conclusions from the pictures of children on games and toys.

8. Look at the sports page of the local newspaper. How much space is given to girls' sports?

9. Have pupils make a list of adjectives they think of when you say "masculine" or "feminine."

10. Ask pupils to make a list of things that only a mother can do for a child and another list for things that only a father can do. Point out that there are few if any entries.

Tools of the Trade

AIM: *To further career awareness.*

This game is played by teams. The object is to guess the tool or object being described and the occupation associated with it. As a class, list several jobs and the objects or tools associated with it. Write one or two per occupation on the chalkboard.

Divide the class into two teams. Copy the job titles on slips of paper, one per slip. Place them in a paper bag. Pass the bag around the room. Each pupil removes one slip.

Underneath the title each pupil writes or copies down the name of the one tool or object he or she associates with the occupation chosen. The teams put their slips of paper in a single bag.

Appoint two captains for each team. One pupil-captain draws a slip of paper out of the opposing team's bag. The other captain goes to the chalkboard. The partner at the board does not know what tool or object his teammate has drawn.

The pupil holding the slip of paper proceeds to describe the tool or object for the student at the board. The board captain sketches the tool/object as it is being described. Only the shape of the object is described, not its nature. For example: for a doctor—draw a rectangle with rounded corners, attach two leader handles to it (doctor's black bag).

The rest of the team members try to guess the tool or object being described and drawn and its related occupation. The pupil describing the tool/object may only respond with a "yes" or "no" to team guesses. If the tool/object is guessed correctly the team gets five points. If tool or object AND occupation are guessed correctly, the team wins ten points. The game continues, alternating teams. The team with the most points wins.

Hiring Practices

AIM: *To acquaint pupils with the procedures for hiring workers.*

Divide the class into two groups. Assign a major industry to each group; for example: air transportation, radio broadcasting, automobile manufacturing, supermarket chain, etc. Each group meets separately to form a company, come up with a corporate name, elect officers, and set up a personnel department. The names may be amusing or serious. The rest of the game is serious.

Because these are new companies, they need to hire new employees. To learn the functions of a personnel department, tell your class a little bit about hiring practices in major companies. Explain such terms as application, interview, training programs, salary, wages, unions, contacts, management, promotions, etc. Each group has its officers decide on the kinds of employees it will require. Guide the children in the selection of those occupations that are essential to the operations of the company. After the officers decide on the kinds of jobs required, the personnel department decides on steps it will take to find and train these workers. The personnel department works up advertisements for classified columns, makes appointments for interviews, conducts interviews, makes decisions about applicants, etc.

Help pupils set up objective criteria for hiring. They may want to draw up their own application blanks. Remind them about federal laws prohibiting discrimination on the basis of age, sex, or race.

While one company is hiring, the other group assumes the role of applicants for positions. A few days later, the roles are reversed. After each group has had chance to "hire" and "be hired" you can hold a general discussion about how a job applicant can make a good impression on a prospective employer.

APPENDIX A

"Where do we go from here?" is a question many teachers ask after they have used our games, puzzles, energizers, and quizzes. We have researched sources for more ideas and activities and would like to share them with you.

The following organizations are constantly updating their list of free and inexpensive materials for teachers. Write a letter to let them know what your needs and interests are. You will be amazed at the great ideas you will receive in the mail!

American Alliance for Health, Physical Education &
   Recreation
1201   16 Street NW
Washington, D.C. 20036

American Textile Manufacturers Institute
Education Department
400 S. Tryon Street
Charlotte, North Carolina 28285

Center for Educational Research
51 Press Building
New York University
New York, N.Y. 10003

Curriculum Development Associates
1211 Connecticut Avenue NW
Washington, D.C. 20036

Curriculum Laboratory
University of Illinois
1210 Springfield Avenue
Urbana, Illinois 61801

Developmental Learning Materials
7440 Natchez Avenue
Niles, Illinois 60648

Education Development Center
55 Chapel Street
Newton, Massachusetts 02160

Environmental Studies for Urban Youth
Evergreen State College
Olympia, Washington 98505

Incentive Publishing Company
Box 12522
Nashville, Tennessee 37212

Institute for Math Studies
Stanford University
Stanford, California 94305

McDonald's Action Packs (Energy)
Box 2594
Chicago, Illinois 60690

Teachers Exchange of San Francisco
600   35th Avenue
San Francisco, California 94121

Teachers Update
Box 205
Saddle River, New Jesey 07458

Varis Associates
Box 893
Hicksville, New York 11802

APPENDIX B

Here are some commercially prepared puzzles and games that may suit your purpose and budget. These companies produce good quality learning materials in the form of games and puzzles that we have personally tested and recommend. A post card will bring you their latest catalog.

Creative Teaching Press
5305 Production Lane
Huntington Beach, California 92649

DM Educational Publications
5502 East Calle del Paisano
Phoenix, Arizona 85018

Frank Schaffer Publications
26616 Indian Peak Road
Palos Verdes Peninsula, California 90274

Good Apple Workshops
Box 299
Carthage, Illinois 62321

Insta Center, Inc.
16745 South Parkside Avenue
Cerritos, California 90701

Jane Ward Co.
1642 S. Beech Street
Lakewood, Colorado 80228

Milton Bradley Co.
Springfield, Massachusetts 01101

Pack-O-Fun
Park Ridge, Illinois 60068

Teachers
Box 398
Manhattan Beach, California 90266

Teaching Resources
100 Boylston Street
Boston, Massachusetts 02116

Trend Enterprises
Box 3073
St. Paul, Minnesota 55165

Ward and Sons
Box 2941
Spartanburg, South Carolina 29304

Wise Owl Publications
Box 3816
Los Angeles, California 90028

INDEX